ADVANCED MENTORING SKILLS

TAKING YOUR CONVERSATIONS TO THE NEXT LEVEL

ANN ROLFE

ISBN 978-0-9803564-8-9

Copyright © 2022 by Ann Rolfe

All rights reserved.

No part of this book may be reproduced in any form or by any electronic or mechanical means, including information storage and retrieval systems, without written permission from the author, except for the use of brief quotations in a book review.

Contact ann@mentoring-works.com

❦ Created with Vellum

CONTENTS

Introduction/Overview   v

PART I
An Approach to Mentoring That Works   1

1. Lead a Mentoring Conversation   3
2. Be Slow To Give Advice   9
3. Build Better Thinking   23
4. Resilience   41

PART II
Critical Skills for Mentors   55

5. Trust   57
6. Advanced Listening   69
7. Good Questions   77
8. Risk Management   89

PART III
Skills for Leader-Mentors   99

9. Leading Learning   101
10. Feedback   111
11. Motivation   123

PART IV
GUIDES

Team Productivity Checklist   135
Brainstorming   139
Force Field Analysis   141
Mindmapping   143

Mentor Master Classes   145
Notes   147
About the Author   149
Also by Ann Rolfe   151

INTRODUCTION/OVERVIEW

Who is This Book For?

You have many opportunities for mentoring in everyday life, at work, in your community. There are both informal and more structured approaches. You may have mentoring conversations, perhaps casually, without thinking of it as mentoring. This book will add value to what you do and how you do it.

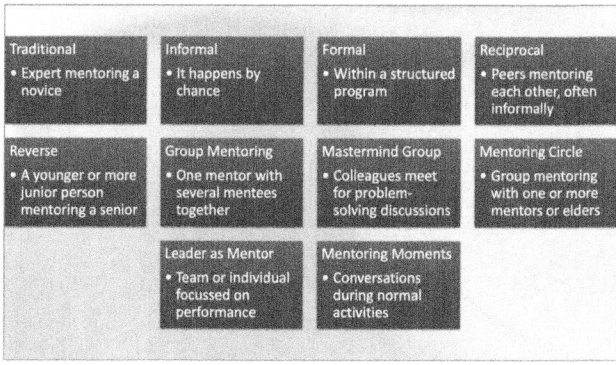

Figure1: Many Ways to Mentor

This book is for you if you are in a mentoring program or a person who mentors others informally.

Perhaps you are a manager or leader and recognise that mentoring is now part of your role.

Maybe people come to you for guidance or advice at work or in the community.

You know mentoring is vital and feel a responsibility to do it well.

I write from over thirty years' experience training mentors and mentees and *Advance Mentoring Skills* complements the information in my previous books: ***Mentoring Mindset, Skills and Tools*** and ***The Mentor's Toolkit for Career Conversations***.

In this book, I'll share what was only previously available in my *Mentor Master Classes* - techniques and tips that even seasoned mentors benefit from. Attendees came from fields as diverse as education and engineering, health and hospitality, construction and communication. They have been professionals, managers, executives and front-line staff.

Buying this book includes **access to view** 12 online *Mentor Master Classes* videos. Here's what participants in my *Mentor Master Classes* have said:

"The knowledge base of the Webinars are giving me a leg up on my thought process as I implement more strategies for this local community of Mentors."

Anthony McCauley, Moore Buddies Mentoring

"Highly motivating to hear such good practical advice that can be applied easily."

Vincenza Steedman

"Very useful and doable."

Margaret Blake

"I like the research that backs up what Ann is saying."

Lynne Sheather, TAFE NSW

"Thank you for sharing the wealth of knowledge for mentors and leaders. Your information was very valuable."

Eva Anderson, Kids R Us Day Care

"A good mix of Ann's personal experience and research stats."

Nisha Divecha

Aim of the Book

My aim in this book is to show you how you can have mentoring conversations more easily, more often, and more effectively.

Content Overview

You may worry about what to say, wonder if you are doing the right thing, or be concerned about what happens when you don't have the answers.

Advanced Skills for Mentors will share an approach to mentoring that works and leave you feeling confident and well equipped.

I'll give you a four-step formula for leading mentoring conversations. So, you'll never have to worry about what to say or do again.

You'll discover why it's better to be slow to give advice and how to decide whether you should or shouldn't offer your own ideas.

You'll see that you don't need to have all the answers! It can be far more valuable to build another person's ability to think critically, creatively and reflectively.

We've all been through a lot the last few years, we need to build resilience - our own as well as others. We also need to look after ourselves and manage risks, so we'll cover these topics too.

We'll go in depth on the critical skills for mentors: building trust, advanced listening and developing good questions.

Because so many managers and leaders now need to mentor their people, we'll look at leading learning in the workplace, using feedback to shape performance and motivation.

Although I frame this book for the workplace, you'll be able to adapt it to your mentoring in the community and perhaps even your family and friends!

Why This Approach to Mentoring Works

I developed my approach to mentoring based on science, sound practice and learning from experts in adult education, career counselling, and coaching.

Positive psychology inspired me. Its emergence at the end of the 20th century expanded the focus of psychology from illness and dysfunction towards well-lived, meaningful and fulfilling lives.

Positive psychology heralded a new era for scientific study and practical applications of psychology for ordinary people. Initiators like Martin Seligman, author of *Learned Optimism*, showed us you don't have to be sick to get better. He introduced us to ways of thinking that enable us to flourish (which is the title of another book he wrote) and emphasised wellbeing, happiness and a meaningful life. Mihaly Csikszentmihaly taught us about "flow" and Donald Clifton pondered, "What if, instead of looking at what's wrong with people, we focused on what's right?"

I've married these concepts with what we know about adult learning, critical thinking and the value of reflection.

This framework for mentoring conversations is based on processes used in strategic planning, classic decision-making and problem-solving, and used in career coaching for decades. It is the key to making your mentoring easy, enjoyable, and effective.

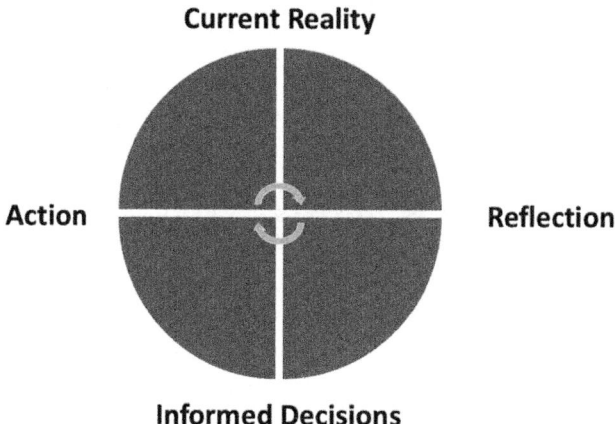

Figure 2: A Framework for Mentoring Conversations

It's not complicated — all you have to do is remember three or four core questions.

It's not rigid — you have complete flexibility.

It is versatile — you'll be able to use it in any type of mentoring situation.

And, it's how I've helped thousands of people become better mentors.

For over three decades, I ran in-person training for mentors in large corporates, government organisations, educational institutions, not-for-profits, industry associations and community groups. Then I took my presentations online. Since 2015, I've offered my clients and the public live webinars. People from all around the world attend. I've turned some of these into shorter video presentations. Your purchase of this book allows you to view my *Mentor Master Classes,* which reflect much of the content in this book. The details and links are in the last section of this book.

I know you'll get real value from your investment in this book. You will expand your knowledge and ability in mentoring and, along the way, become a better communicator. This will benefit your relationships at work, at home, and in life.

Author's Note

Greetings from Australia. I write in Australian English so readers used to American spellings may notice organisation spelled with an s instead of a z, colour and behaviour with a u and other words used or spelled slightly differently. These are not mistakes, but correct practice down-under.

Enjoy!

Ann

Ann Rolfe, Founder Mentoring Works.

PART I
AN APPROACH TO MENTORING THAT WORKS

1
LEAD A MENTORING CONVERSATION

What is a Mentoring Conversation?

Have you had the experience of talking to someone who really listened to you? Someone who said little, but was clearly attentive, interested, and supportive as you shared your thoughts. You felt heard, and you felt better. Perhaps you solved a problem — with or without their input. Perhaps you gained insight — understanding, an "Ah ha!" moment, a realisation that bubbled up from inside you. Maybe you came to a decision — or at least discovered choices available to you, or you resolved to research alternatives and opportunities. This is what I would call a mentoring conversation.

> *A mentoring conversation is one where:*
> *people are safe to explore thoughts and feelings.*
> *They use critical, creative and above all reflective thinking to*
> *gain insight and generate possible options.*
> *They make informed choices*
> *as they decide on goals and actions.*
> *They are assisted, as needed, to plan the way forward, and*
> *they are supported and encouraged*
> *as they implement their plan.*

Figure 3: A Definition of Mentoring

A mentoring conversation is a dialogue, a two-way flow of communication. It encourages the mentee to do about 80% of the talking. The mentor leads the conversation by creating a safe space, then asking questions that enable the mentee to open their mouth to speak and, in doing so, open their mind.

We have a conscious and a subconscious mind. The conscious mind is where we deliberately think about things. We are conscious of thoughts that float through our awareness. Yet there is a lot going on below the surface: ideas, attitudes, and subconscious influences. These shape our actions at least as much and probably more than our conscious decisions.

Counsellors talk about their client's "presenting problem", that is what's top of mind when the client begins to talk. They know this is not the entire issue and it will take time to create safety, use good questions and exceptional listening to get down to it. While mentors are definitely not psychotherapists, we need to keep in mind that the mentee's first comments are their rationale for coming to you and we will help most if we explore beyond the superficial. Here's how.

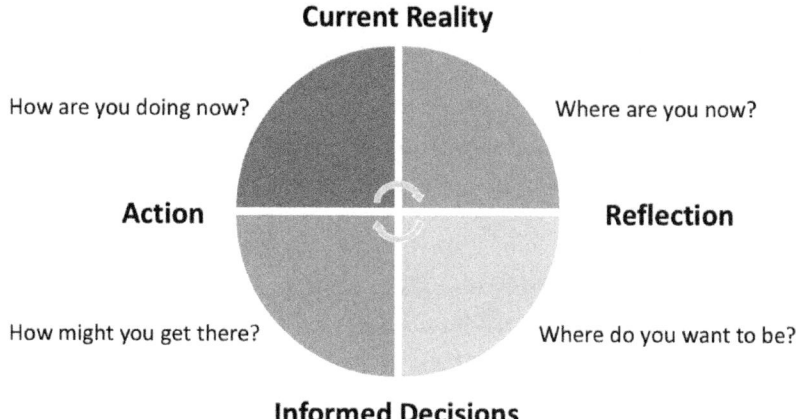

Figure 4: Framework with Four Questions

I've laid the framework for a mentoring conversation out like an analog clock face, where we begin at the twelve o'clock position. We'll move in a clockwise fashion, first talking about their current reality, getting the person to reflect on the situation, issue, or topic they want to discuss. Then the dialogue looks at the future and helps them make informed decisions about it. We may then assist them in setting goals and plan actions. Finally, we'll support them as they take action.

Although I've suggested a clockwise cycle through this process, and I'll continue that as I explain each of the four elements in more detail, keep in mind that in a real mentoring conversation, you'll likely skip back and forth many times. Although I talk about *the* mentoring conversation, it is more likely to be a series of conversations over time. You can't rush it and you need to remain flexible! Mentoring is about enabling people to decide for themselves, and set goals that are right for them. The framework provides a supporting structure for you and for them.

Four Questions

I built the mentoring conversation on 4 questions, I call them the "Umbrella Questions". These are not the questions you ask the mentee, but the questions you hold in your mind. You frame questions most appropriate for the person and the situation.

In the noon to three o'clock position, we want the mentee to explore their thoughts and feelings about the topic they have raised. We want them to reflect; we want to draw them out. If we are successful, they will literally think out loud. We will use open-ended questions to get them started, but essentially what you're trying to find out is: where are you now? You want the mentee to reflect on what's going on, clearly understand the current reality, problem, situation, or event. We want to explore their thoughts and feelings, so we're going to use open-ended questions.

We'll start broadly, for example:

"What's on your mind today?"

"What would you like to talk about?"

"What's on your agenda?"

And then home in on the issue.

It is quite possible that when they reflect on the situation, they'll realise that there are deeper issues that need to be considered. The question on top of their mind is not the actual issue. Freud said "the mind is like an iceberg, it floats with one-seventh of its bulk above water." There's a lot going on below the surface of our conscious mind. We are not trying to psychoanalyse our mentee, but we want to increase their awareness of their own values, priorities, preferences and motivation, which may linger below the surface.

We want them to talk so we'll listen and use minimal responses like "mm hm", "uh huh", "go on" to encourage them to keep going.

We might need to probe gently with phrases like:

"Can you say a little more about..."

"Would you expand on that..."

"Perhaps you'd like to tell me how..."

We'll use reflective listening to help them clarify their thoughts, to check our understanding or summarise. We mights say:

"So what you're saying is..."

"What I'm hearing is..."

"From your point of view..."

Then paraphrase or repeat back to them succinctly what they've said.

They say Archimedes yelled "Eureka!" and ran naked out into the street after a flash of insight gave him the answer to a problem while he was in the bath! But, no matter how excited they are, we want mentees to make informed decisions about what they do, not simply leap into action.

Some mentees may not know what they really want or what they're capable of. So, our job is to help them generate options and possibilities.

After establishing "where they are now" we want to move to "where do they want to be?" Again, this is the umbrella question, the one you hold in your mind, as you formulate an appropriate questions for this mentee.

In this part of the conversation, you are comparing and contrasting the current situation with an ideal one. You will continue using open questions, minimal responses, perhaps gentle probing, and reflective listening. But we have an additional aim now. We want them to make informed decisions before they take action. They may need more information and their first action may be research.

When the mentee is well informed and ready, the conversation proceeds so that they can decide on their goals and plan actions. The next umbrella question is "how might you get there?"

You won't have to worry about what to say or do next if you remember these three questions. Your question will always be a variation of one of these.

Most of the planning should come from the mentee. So as much as possible, keep asking them questions. Limit, but don't withhold your own input. Don't be afraid to send them away with research tasks. They can go away to think about things and come back to you with ideas to discuss.

It will be sometime later, when they've done something based on your conversation, that they'll come back so you can talk about follow-through and adjustment. Lead a review of their action and outcomes. Another umbrella question frames this conversation. It might be something like "how are you doing now?"

Now you have the four umbrella questions, the framework for any mentoring conversation. You might like to pause and jot down some questions under these headings that would work for you.

Where are you now?

Where do you want to be?

How might you get there?

How are you doing now?

2

BE SLOW TO GIVE ADVICE

All the current expert advice on giving advice is don't!

Of course, it is easy to argue that people seek a mentor because they want advice, and while that may be true, giving advice is the *least* helpful thing you can do for them.

Not giving advice is difficult to swallow because you're naturally action-oriented. Your work may require you to solve problems, come up with solutions quickly, and make decisions. If you're a manager, a leader or in a position of authority, you may be used to directing or organising others, but mentoring takes a different approach.

I don't say *never* give advice, but make it a last resort. So, first we'll look at 10 reasons not to give advice, then I'll provide suggestions of what to do instead. Finally, I'll offer some techniques if you must give advice because often it's not what you do, but how you do it. And yes, the irony is not lost on me that all of this adds up to giving advice!

10 Reasons Not to Give Advice

> 1. Sometimes people just need to vent, they don't want advice
> 2. It implies they are incompetent and is demotivating
> 3. It can be perceived as criticism and lead to self-justification and resistance
> 4. Feeling judged and defensive is a barrier to communication
> 5. It shifts the power dynamic in a relationship
> 6. You don't have all the information
> 7. People are unique, what works for you may not work for them
> 8. It robs them of the opportunity to learn and grow
> 9. It can build dependence and reduce self-responsibility
> 10. You're not the one who must face the consequences

Figure 5: 10 Reasons Not to Give Advice

1. Sometimes people just want to vent, they don't want advice. Ever chatted with a friend or a loved one and told them about a challenge you'd had? When, with words barely out of your mouth, they started telling what you *should* have done, what *they* would have done, or what your next move must be? Recall that experience and how you felt. If you can't remember a time like that, notice your inner response next time it happens — it definitely will.

Everybody needs to vent, to tell others about experiences good and bad, to "let off steam", "get it off our chest", but that doesn't mean that we need solutions. People are not always seeking help, they may simply need to be heard. People often need to be validated — to feel that what they are thinking and feeling is normal.

2. Advice implies they are incompetent, and it is demotivating. Telling people what to do suggests they don't know, can't figure out, or lack the capability to do something different to get a better result. That's why it can feel insulting when people give unsolicited advice. It's different when you go to a doctor, lawyer or landscape gardener. You're paying for expert advice and you're seeking professional input in a field you know less about. Payment for advice balances the relationship.

In his book, *Drive: The Surprising Truth About What Motivates Us*, Daniel Pink explains the secret to performance and satisfaction. Decades of research have identified that humans need and strive for autonomy—the desire to direct our own lives; mastery—the ability to learn and create; and purpose—a reason for living and endeavour. So, telling people what to do takes away *everything* that motivates them.

3. Advice can be perceived as criticism and lead to self-justification and resistance. You give advice because you want to help; you want the person to know what they can do, or how they can change, to get a better outcome, but it usually backfires. When we hear someone tell us we need to do something different, we often subconsciously feel like we're being told we're wrong, bad, or stupid.

Criticism is painful. Neuroscientists have discovered that emotional pain feels as bad as physical pain. We all have a strong desire to avoid pain if we can. Therefore, you may find the person receiving the advice explaining themselves and reasons they had to do what they did. Being unable to see options is disempowering and the opposite of what you want. Self-justification also entrenches their beliefs. It narrows their mind instead of opening it to new ideas. As their attitude hardens, they'll tell you all the reasons your suggestions won't work and they'll resist change.

4. Feeling judged and defensive is a barrier to communication. There is a primitive part of our brain primed to defend against any threat. It helped the survival of the earliest humans because it triggers the flight/fight/freeze reaction. It's fast because life depended upon it and it reacts to emotional as well as physical threat before conscious thought, logic, and reason can respond.

Judgement is one of the most threatening feelings there is. Automatically, the brain leaps into defensive action. Neurochemicals flood the brain to prepare for battle, to run away or hide. People hear differently, see differently, process differently, and behave differently. They are on guard, barriers come up and they are likely to:

- **Fight**—resist, argue, justify, attack
- **Flight**—change the subject, leave, ignore
- **Freeze**—like a rabbit in the headlights, shut down, unable to move, think, respond.

Any of these reactions severely limits communication.

5. Advice shifts the power dynamic in a relationship. In mentoring, we strive to have an open and balanced relationship. We are adults with neither exercising power over the other. In giving advice, one is taking control and thus gains higher status.

When one gives advice, it lowers the status of the other. It lowers self-esteem, self-confidence and self-efficacy—the belief that we can achieve our goals, overcome setbacks, or master tasks. Just as the brain constantly scans for threats, it also weighs our status in relation to other people.

We instinctively understand the importance of status. High-status individuals get more. Whether it's food, money, sex, the corner office, the car or parking spot or better assignments at work. The brain is constantly evaluating our status compared to others. The bigger the disparity between our status and someone else's, the harder it is to communicate. Imagine an ordinary citizen trying to chat with Royalty or the President or Prime Minister.

6. You don't have all the information. You can't know all the facts of a situation, let alone all the background, thoughts, feelings or life-experience of people involved. Your point of view is limited to the information you have and you don't have the entire story. In life, there are very few simple clear-cut cause-and-effect problems. Most have multiple interconnected variables. You may have it wrong.

7. People are unique. What works for you may not work for them. What you would or could do in a situation depends on a whole range of factors, but you are not them. They don't see the world the way you see it. They have their own personality, knowledge and skills that differ from yours. Their needs and values are not the same as yours.

We mentor because we want to empower people to make their own choices that are right for them. We do not want to create a clone or transplant our mind over theirs.

8. Advice robs them of the opportunity to learn and grow. One of the most important ways we develop is by figuring things out. Thinking "what if..." considering options, searching for information, deciding and planning for ourselves. If you give people solutions, it short-circuits their problem-solving process. They miss out on the sense of mastery you get when you come up with your own answer and apply it, a process that strengthens you, makes you more competent and confident.

9. Advice can build dependence and reduce self-responsibility. It's unhealthy when people don't have the opportunity to think for themselves, when they run to you with every question, or they need your validation for decisions. They may remain tethered to you. They will feel little satisfaction with results and may blame you when things don't work out. Because they don't make the decisions, they won't take responsibility. They won't have ownership and there will be little commitment.

10. You're not the one who must face the consequences. The bottom line is that we each must take responsibility for our choices and actions. That's what being an adult means. We recognise that decisions have consequences, behaviour produces results. Inaction has ramifications too. You can't dictate what they should do. They have to use their own best judgment because they have to live with the outcomes.

What to do Instead

You can be an excellent mentor, friend, parent, colleague if you train yourself to hold back from giving advice—even when asked for it! Talk less and listen more and watch your relationships blossom.

If someone comes to you with an issue, listen! Use the minimal responses, gentle probing and reflective listening mentioned in the previous chapter with advanced listening and good questions detailed in later chapters, to let them talk and feel heard. There's so much more you can do with a mentoring conversation.

Elicit	Their thoughts and feelings about the situation
Focus	On their values and needs regarding the situation
Identify	Their goals or preferred outcomes for the situation
Clarify	The issues impacting on the situation
Explore	Options, possible alternatives to achieve their preferred outcome
Discuss	Actions they could take, things to stop doing, and what they might do differently to move toward their desired outcome and consequences of actions and inaction
Obtain	Commitment to their next steps

Figure 6: Instead of Advice

Elicit their thoughts and feelings about the situation. In the mentoring conversation, you first aim to have them reflect on their current reality, meaning what's going on from their point of view, their perspective on the situation. A person's perception — how they see the world and events in their life — is shaped by their thoughts, feelings, previous experience and imagination. So it's important to find out what's going on for them.

You might begin with:

"What's on your mind?"

Now you want to draw them out. Don't rush them, allow pauses and silence that let them process, so that what they think and how they feel can emerge. Be respectfully curious. Do not judge or even critique what they say. Remember, what *you* think is not important, at this stage, it's about them bringing information up into their conscious awareness. Regard their first comments as the tip of the iceberg, because emotions, beliefs and assumptions frequently lie below the surface in their subconscious.

Not everyone wants to talk about their thoughts, much less their feelings, but these are the true drivers of actions and results. We like to think we are rational creatures motivated by logic, but beliefs—what we tell our self is good/bad right/wrong, what we *must* do or how we *should* be treated, and emotions—our affective response (reaction generated by feelings) are what most influence behaviour and our satisfaction in the world, or lack of it.

Focus on their values regarding the situation. We like to think that we share common values, that most of us think the same things are important, but that's only true up to a point. Our upbringing in our family, our culture, and wider society will shape our outlook, but we are individuals. Our inner world and experiences make each of us unique. This means we have an inner code, a set of beliefs that drive and inhibit us. Mine is going to be a little or a lot different to yours and so is each person's that you mentor. Another reason that what's right for you may not be right for them. Ask them:

"What makes this important to you?"

You'll want to use reflective listening to summarise or paraphrase what you're hearing. There's likely several different values and beliefs at play. Some may even conflict with each other. For example, they may have a strong desire to do a good job, but deadlines and pressure from above force them to cut corners and do work that is less than perfect.

Identify their goals or preferred outcomes for the situation. When a person seeks mentoring, it is because they want something to improve in their life. They may need to vent their frustration, express their unhappiness, or lament their circumstances, but you can't let them wallow in self-pity. Sooner or later, you're going to lead the conversation towards to what they want *instead* of the current situation so that they can decide what to do about it. Don't shift gears too quickly. They need to have had enough time to thoroughly articulate what's on their mind, but when you gauge the time is right, summarise the issue and follow up with a question.

"From what you've told me, I understand X is a major concern for you?" Pause for confirmation. *"So, tell me, how would you prefer things to be?"*

They may resist, wanting to continue to vent. After all, so seldom do we get uninterrupted time to be heard, validated and understood that once we do, we may not want to stop! So, let them have a little more time, then rephrase your question:

"What would the ideal situation be, from your point of view?"

You want to facilitate as vivid a description of their goal as you can.

"Paint me a picture of what that looks like?"

Continue reflective listening until you believe they are clear on what they want.

Clarify the issues affecting the situation. Life is complicated. Many factors and circumstances influence people's behaviour, perceptions and results. There is seldom a single cause-and-effect relationship. More often, it's a bunch of interactive elements that produce the situation that is the subject of your conversation. You can ask some questions to explore these such as

"What do you think are the major influences on this situation?"

"What else might be a factor causing this?"

I've included an explanation and guide to the use of Force Field Analysis later in this book to identify multiple factors that can assist or inhibit the achievement of goals.

Explore options. Help them find viable alternatives to achieve their preferred outcome.

"Let's brainstorm some ideas about what you might do to change the situation."

Discuss actions they could take, things they could stop doing, and what they might do differently to move toward their desired outcome and the consequences of action and inaction.

"What could you do that might change the situation for the better?"

"Is there anything you are doing now that if you stopped, would make things better?"

"Is there anything else that you could do differently for a positive result?"

Get commitment to their next steps. Have them summarise their actions and the time-frame for them. Get them to talk about the benefits or reasons for each planned step. Let them know that the two of you will review progress next time you meet.

"So what are the things you'll do before we next meet?"

"Great! We'll talk about how that went next time."

So When Do You Give Advice?

Mentoring is dynamic — it moves and changes in response to the mentee's needs. The diagram below shows a vertical line. At one end, you elicit with your questions and listening and the other you impart, share your knowledge and experience. Likewise, the horizontal line illustrates that on the one hand, you support your mentee with encouragement and validation. On the other, you challenge their thinking by providing a different perspective. Think of each line in the diagram as a spectrum that your dialogue can move along. You can provide information can help them make informed decisions, and a different perspective can expand their thinking. Both these outcomes are important parts of mentoring. However, you earn the right to impart and challenge by first eliciting and supporting. If you listen well, you are more likely to be listened to. The support you've given your mentee with encouragement and validation, rather than judgement, will allow them to feel safe when they're challenged with a different view. Go too fast to impart or challenge and they will be defensive and resistant.

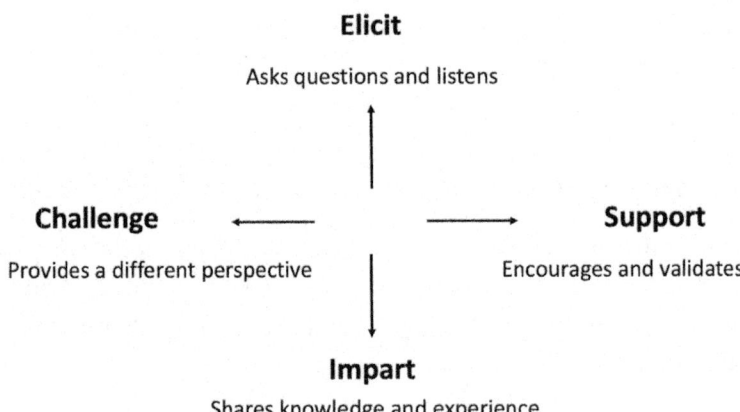

Figure 7: The Mentoring Dynamic

Share Knowledge and Experience

We want a mentee to make informed decisions, by definition, that means they need to have valid and reliable information as their basis. Often, once you've unpacked the issues, it will become clear that they need more information before they decide what to do. There are three places they can get that information:

1. **Within.** Reflecting on their own knowledge and experience, developing self-awareness, thoughts, and feelings.

2. **External Sources.** Reading, researching, consulting experts, looking at data.
3. **You.** Asking about your experience, finding out what you know.

The time to share your knowledge and experience is:

- After you've drawn out their knowledge and noticed gaps.
- When you have relevant, important information that will make a difference
- If it is appropriate to share something they may not otherwise learn

Provide a Different Perspective

Each of us has our own ways of seeing the world. Even when people experience the same events, their views, opinions and responses can be quite different. One of the most valuable things you can do as a mentor is to enable your mentee to see a different perspective. You don't want to tell them their views are wrong; you don't want to debate or argue; you simply want to help them see more possibilities. As a rule of thumb: **Listen before you ask, ask before you tell.**

You can expand their thinking by asking questions like:

"How do you imagine others view that?"

"Is there another way to interpret that?"

"What other points of view could there be on that?"

After you have stimulated their thinking, you may still wish to respectfully offer your point of view.

Giving Advice

When you *do* give advice, remember the adage: "It's not just what you do, it's the way that you do it."

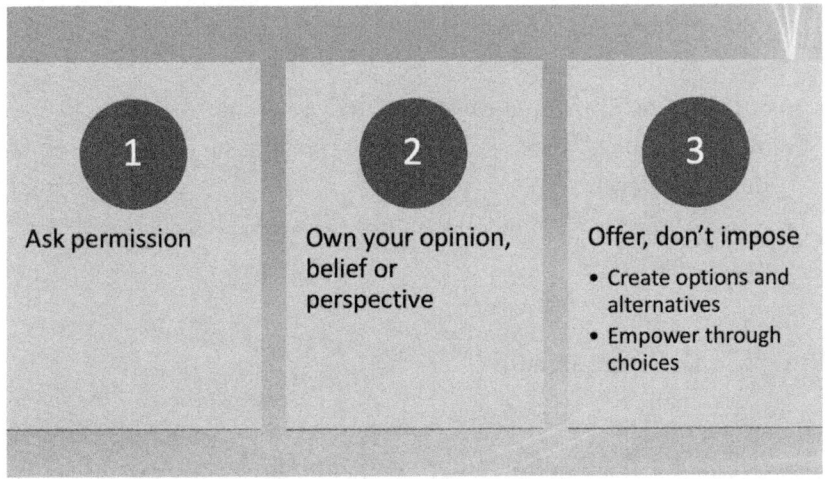

Figure 8: Giving Advice

Ask permission before you give any advice. This might take the form of:

"May I make a suggestion?"

"Would you like me to share my observations?"

"I have a different take on that. Are you open to hearing it?"

It is important to own our opinions, beliefs or views because they are based on what we've been taught, the information that we have access to and the way our personal experience, preconceived ideas and assumptions shape our thinking. We must recognise that opinions, beliefs, or views are not necessarily true or false, even when based on facts. Frequently, we form our ideas with many influences at play. It's useful to preface statements to signal you are offering your opinion, belief, or point of view.

"In my opinion"

"I believe/think/feel"

"From my point of view"

A key to giving advice is to offer but not impose it. The mentee should not feel compelled to do what you suggest. So, make your advice one of several options or alternatives.

"One way to handle this might be..."

"Another tactic could be..."

"Let's brainstorm some different ways to deal with this."

Notice the words: *may, could, might*. This terminology implies possibility, alternatives rather than instruction.

People are empowered when they have choice. Adults are motivated by autonomy and more committed to actions of their choice. So, brainstorm many options for action or generate at least two or three through your conversation, then encourage the mentee to choose the most suitable for them.

Ensure that you discuss possible consequences of actions and inaction before they decide what they'll do. Set a time to review progress, where they may confirm and continue their plan, or change and adjust actions.

3

BUILD BETTER THINKING

You can do so much good when you help your mentee develop thinking skills. They can:

- Improve their career
- Increase their well-being
- Contribute to a meaningful life

There are four types of thinking that are an asset to mentees.

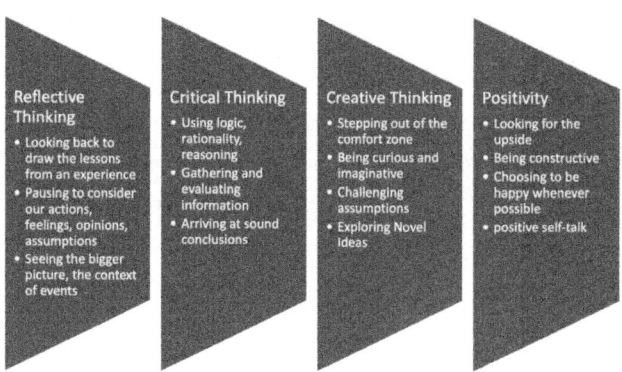

Figure 10: Four Types of Thinking

By facilitating reflective thinking, you'll show them how to leverage their past for a better future. With critical thinking, they'll gain better judgement. Creative thinking encourages innovation and new ideas, and positivity builds resilience.

Reflective Thinking

Reflective thinking is the art of looking for the lessons life offers. It is the discipline to respond after pausing to think, rather than simply reacting. It is the skill of making sense of events that are complex.

Because people are naturally action-oriented, we feel a need to do something rather than stay still. We are often busy, overloaded with multiple demands, and stressed, so we may not take time out to reflect. One gift mentoring brings is the timeout for a conversation aimed at increasing reflective thinking.

They say hindsight is twenty-twenty vision in the rear-view mirror, but looking back can provide powerful learning that we can apply in the present and future. When we reflect, we review what happened, what went well and what didn't, why it happened, how we feel about it, what we'd repeat or do differently in the future.

Reflection is not about berating ourselves for past mistakes. It's about *learning* from our failures and our successes. Then using the lessons to improve. Reflection allows us to develop self-awareness and empower ourselves. It increases our choices and ability to change.

As a mentor, you help your mentee understand past actions and outcomes. They can explore their reactions, feelings, and emotions. You can encourage your mentee to reflect on their experience by asking questions. For example:

"Tell me about what happened?"

"How do you feel about that?"

"What worked well?"

"What didn't work so well?"

"What did you learn from that?"

"What could you do in future?"

Sometimes you'll deal with events that could have gone better. Your attitude needs to be accepting. Implied judgment or criticism will trigger defensiveness and close the learning opportunity. Remind the mentee that it is impossible to change the past, but you have power to make new choices in the present and take different actions in the future.

You'll also have your mentee reflect on situations where they have applied their strengths and produced positive outcomes. Then have them consider how they can apply those strengths in the present and future. This not only provides them with practical strategies, it builds their confidence. If they have no positive example of their own, you can ask them to think about how others have approached similar challenges and figure out ways to do something equivalent.

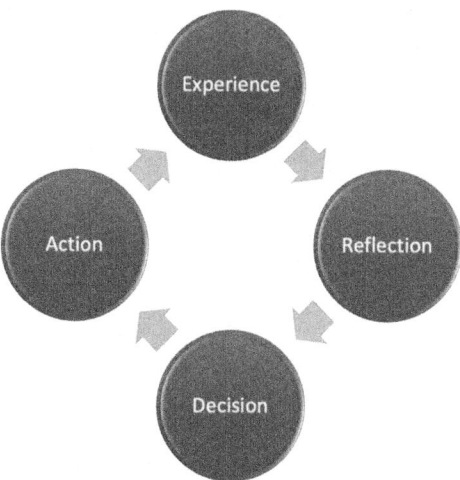

Figure 11: The Learning Cycle

Thinking is part of a learning cycle. The mentee reflects to get the learning from an experience. They plan how to apply that learning in the present or future. Then they act on their plan, which creates a fresh experience. They observe and review this, repeating the learning cycle for continuous improvement.

Critical Thinking

The experience of the COVID-19 pandemic showed how much we need critical thinking. The pervasiveness of polarising opinions and misinformation has been as dangerous as the virus itself.

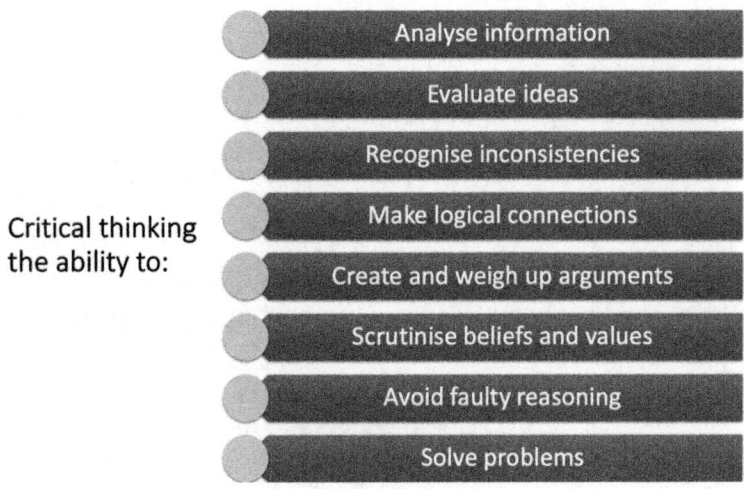

Figure 12: Critical Thinking

People jumped to conclusions based on false, shaky, or non-existent evidence. Some people convincingly delivered wrong or misleading information in the all forms of media, and in-person. They passed off opinions as facts. Newspapers, politicians, gossips and well-meaning but ill-informed people have been doing this forever. However, because of the internet, the proliferation and speed of information means it's never been more important to think critically and exercise sound judgment.

In the workplace, lack of critical thinking is a problem. It can lead to poor policy and decision-making, business or personal failure and vulnerability to manipulation. In addition, critical thinking is fundamental to democracy and science and promotes creativity. Critical thinking means systematically processing information, so we understand things better and make better decisions.

How to Get Mentees to Think Critically

If you've become skilled in leading reflective conversations, you've already modelled and started them in the right direction through introspection. Add to that by developing their:

- **Self-awareness**—help mentees understand their own thinking process and how tiredness, bias, emotional state and lack of attention reduce efficacy.
- **Focus**—we like to think we can multi-task, but we can't. Neuroscientists have shown that in attempts to multi-task, the brain flits back and forth between tasks, reducing effectiveness in each. Some have calculated a drop of 10-20 IQ points when people try to multi-task. Help mentees value and practice concentration, reduce distractions, have the discipline to read long-form and listen well.
- **Attention to Evidence**—ensure mentees distinguish between fact and opinion, credible sources and untrustworthy ones. Help them understand that click-bait is manipulation. It aims to sell you something, be it a product, a political view or conspiracy theory, or it's a ploy to harvest your personal data.
- **Ability to Spot Omissions**—cherry picking is common in putting an argument. This is where we choose some facts and ignore others that do not support the case. Help mentees look for the holes.
- **Systematically Question**—**have** them check the reliability and validity of the information, its source, and the motivation of people behind it. Ask who gains from it?

I'd also recommend that you introduce mentees to Robert Cialdini's classic, *Influence: The Psychology of of Persuasion* because it explains the science behind the key techniques of influence:

- Reciprocation—if I do you a favour, you owe me one
- Commitment and Consistency—a small initial commitment can lead to a larger one consistent with the first.
- Social Proof—if others are doing it, we are more likely to do so too.
- Liking—we like people like us, we like people who compliment us or help us and we're more likely to trust or buy from them.
- Authority—we'll follow the lead of people we believe to be knowledgeable and credible.
- Scarcity—we value anything in limited supply more highly. We suffer from FOMO (fear of missing out).

Creative Thinking

We often think creativity is a gift associated with talented artists. It's a label we apply to painters, sculptors, writers, musicians, craftspeople, designers, architects, brilliant inventors, and people who make great breakthroughs in science, entrepreneurs in business and technology. However, each of us has creativity. It is an ability that we use a little or a lot. It is a skill that we can develop.

As a mentor, you want your mentee to be creative in finding new ideas, different ways of approaching issues, and innovative strategies for getting the outcomes they want.

People often talk about creative thinking as "thinking outside the box." The "box" they speak of is the boundary that surrounds what we know. The "box" is a comfortable, secure place in our mind where we can speak confidently about what we are sure of. Creativity means stepping out of that comfort zone, into the unknown, courageously admitting we don't know what we don't know, being humble enough to realise there is more beyond our current awareness.

You want your mentee to be curious, positive, and imaginative. They may need to challenge assumptions, questions beliefs and suspend judgement so that they can entertain and explore novel ideas before evaluating them.

How to Encourage Creative Thinking

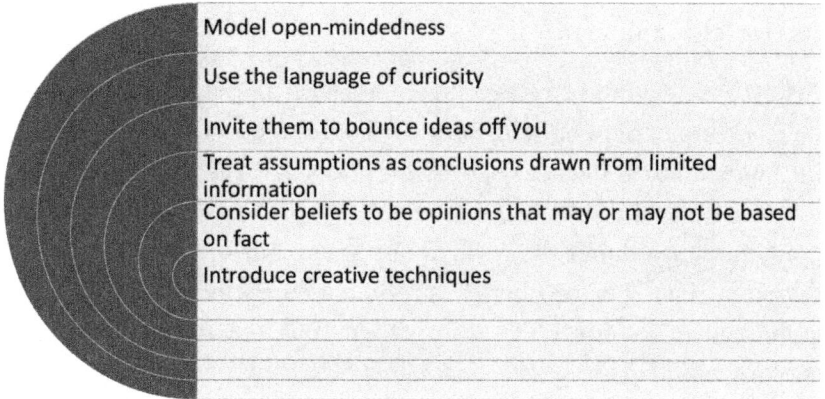

Figure 13: Encourage Creative Thinking

You are a role model for your mentee. What you say, the way you say it, your attitudes, and your behaviours provide examples they may follow. Show them your open-mindedness by suspending judgement, being willing to accept ideas—you don't have to agree with an idea or be untruthful, you can say something like *"I can see how you might think that,"* or *"from your perspective it certainly looks that way,"* sincerely and with integrity.

Show your curiosity. Use phrases like *"I wonder," "let's imagine,"* to explore possibilities. Avoid prescriptive terms like "must" or "should" use "might" or "could" that imply there are options.

Mentees often describe their mentor as a sounding board. They value someone they can bounce ideas off. Your creative use of questions will enable them to expand and evaluate their own thinking. Do this before offering input or feedback.

It is very common to treat assumptions and beliefs as facts. However, an assumption is a conclusion drawn from information. That information may be incomplete or incorrect. A belief is an opinion that may or may not be based on fact. People develop assumptions and beliefs from a very young age. In western cultures, some adults conspire to encourage children to believe in Santa Claus, the Tooth Fairy and the Easter Bunny. Many other beliefs that could be let go survive into adulthood.

Always take care to be respectful when challenging assumptions and beliefs. Some are long held, cherished, and unquestioned. It is up to the individual to decide if an assumption or belief serves them or limits them and if they are ready to change it. Most kids cope with a gradual realisation of the truth about Santa, but the revelation shatters some. Each person cherishes certain assumptions and beliefs. As a mentor, it's not our job to destroy them, but to equip the mentee to explore them.

Creative techniques that you may find helpful in mentoring include brainstorming, force-field analysis and mindmapping. These are outlined in the guides at the back of this book.

You can also encourage your mentee to:

- **Take time to think**—quality thinking requires time, but in a busy life, we may not see spending time with our thoughts as productive. We need to get over our action-bias and value thinking, reflecting, planning for the vital contributors they are.
- **Muse**—make it a habit to ponder, ruminate, contemplate. This can be done with others or alone. You can read fiction or non-fiction, watch movies or documentaries, or study

subjects like art, philosophy, sociology, history or science. Almost any subject can give you pause for thought.
- **Daydream**—teachers frown upon daydreaming and letting the mind wander in a classroom. However, a childlike curiosity, imagination and daydreaming foster creativity.
- **Practice artistic hobbies**—artistic, physical, or even routine activities often free the mind to wander. The subconscious is always processing information in the background and will often throw a new idea into consciousness while you are otherwise occupied.
- **Be in nature**—this calms and refreshes you. The environment helps reflection, musing, daydreaming, and meditation.
- **"Sleep on it"**—this allows time, usually overnight, for the mind to process information. A wise strategy when consider a decision or problem. There are many stories of inventions, solutions and creative ideas in dreams, or dawning soon after waking. I always defer a really important decision or response until I have slept on it. When I wake, I have either reconsidered and chosen a different path or become more confident in the original decision.

Positivity

Positive psychology has to be one of the best advancements in human development. Positive psychology heralded a new era for scientific study. It provided practical applications of psychology for ordinary people. Previously, the focus of the science was on helping or curing sick people. Initiators of positive psychology, like Martin Seligman, author of *Learned Optimism*, showed us you don't have to be sick to get better! He shifted the focus to improving the quality of life for all of us. This means an emphasis on wellbeing, happiness and a meaningful life.

Another pioneer, Mihaly Csikszentmihaly, taught us about "flow". Donald Clifton pondered: "What if, instead of looking at what's wrong with people, we focused on what's right?" More recently, Barbara Fredrickson's team analysed positivity and Carol Dweck researched the growth mindset.

Positivity is a state of mind that is beneficial to:

- Relationships
- Health
- Resilience
- Personal and professional development.

Positivity means seeing, saying and doing helpful, constructive or happy things. It can mean changing some of our habitual thinking and self-talk. That doesn't mean we have to view the world with rose-coloured glasses; we need to have a realistic awareness of negativity, but there's a tipping point. Concentrated negativity leads to failure, but the right balance of positivity and negativity enables people to flourish. The research has found that we need heart-felt positive emotions to outweigh negative ones at a ratio of at least 3:1.

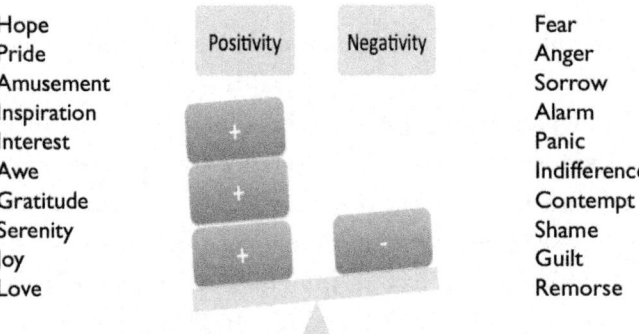

Figure 14: The Magic Ratio

As a mentor, there are many ways you can strengthen your mentee's positivity, including:

- Check self-talk and the tame the inner critic
- Establish what is within their control and what is not
- Build a growth mindset
- Focus on talents and strengths development
- Look for positives

Unfortunately, many people cannot reach even the tipping point of 3:1. In tough times, it can be hard to see beauty, difficult to experience enjoyment, challenging to find what's good. It is wise to accept unhappiness. Grief comes to us all. It is not always appropriate to look on the bright side, it can be annoying and make people feel that their sadness is trampled on. However, most of the time, it's worth cultivating the habit of looking for positives and feelings of gratitude. We can take pleasure in the smallest of things, we can seek them every day, and help others notice them too.

Self-Talk and the Inner Critic

The way we talk about ourselves and to ourselves has a powerful impact. Too often, our language is self-denigrating, negative and full of frequently unwarranted self-criticism. Negative thoughts and feelings which are usually accumulated from our environment—parents, schoolteachers, peers, or other people we listen to—can become ingrained. Such limiting beliefs rob us of confidence and stymie growth.

If limiting beliefs are holding the mentee back, you'll want to help them shift their perspective.

Recall The Mentoring Dynamic (described in chapter 2). Your approach balances elicit and support with impart and challenge. You'll need to have developed rapport and trust and walk the path gently and respectfully as you lead any conversation about self-talk. A mentee with an inner critic doesn't need another on the outside, and if they become defensive, it will be a barrier to communication. Instead, you can help them realise that the beliefs and the opinions expressed by their inner critic are not reality. They can change negative self-talk to something more constructive and update old beliefs.

The aim of mentors is to help mentees develop a realistic and rational view of themselves and their capabilities. Listen to the words they use and their inference when talking about themselves. Some words are global generalisations. They take one or two examples and form a belief based on this limited information. Listen for words or phrases that show a global generalisation, like: "always", "never", "everyone". You can counter this habit with a simple question and gentle correction. For example:

Mentee: *"I always fail in interviews."*

Mentor: *"Always?"* (Curious tone, enquiring look, followed by silence)

Mentee: *"I certainly blew the last one!"*

Mentor: *"So, it may be fair to say the last one didn't go well, and we can talk about that and what you can do differently, but I'm thinking that saying you always fail is an over-generalisation. After all, you interviewed successfully and won your current job."* (Silent pause, expectant look)

Mentee: *"Well... that's true."*

Mentor: *"And you've successfully interviewed for previous jobs."*

Mentee: *"Yes, but... the more recent ones... I've failed."*

Mentor: *"OK. I think it would be useful to look at the differences between the ones where you won the job and the recent ones where you didn't. What do you think?"*

Self-criticism can be quite ingrained and take a while to change. However, with patience and persistence, most people can tame their inner critic. You can reduce the effects of an inner critic, limiting beliefs, and negative self-talk by helping the mentee:

- Recognise their inner critic in action—call it out
- Use rational thinking to evaluate how much truth is or is not, in the criticism
- Choose more constructive ways to self-critique for self-improvement
- Practice compassion (for others and themself)
- Learn to change self-talk

Develop your own repertoire of questions and phrases to use in this type of conversations. Here are some samples:

"Sounds like you may have an over-active inner critic giving you a hard time?"

"Is that really true, or something your inner critic tells you?"

"Perhaps that was so in the past, but could it be different in the future?"

"Can I ask what led you to that conclusion?"

"I'm curious to know what prompted that opinion?"

"I'm wondering if there's another way to look at that?"

"Isn't that a bit harsh? How would a good friend more kindly give you that feedback?"

"Self-critique can be useful for improvement, but criticism seldom is. How could you think about that in a more constructive way?"

The Control Principle

In his classic book *The Seven Habits of Highly Effective People*, the late Stephen Covey described a very empowering concept: the control principle. The illustration on the next page shows an outer circle, the circle of concern. This represents those things a person cares about but can do little or nothing about. The inner circle is the circle of control, those aspects that the person has most influence over. We have most control of what we say, what we do, and what we think.

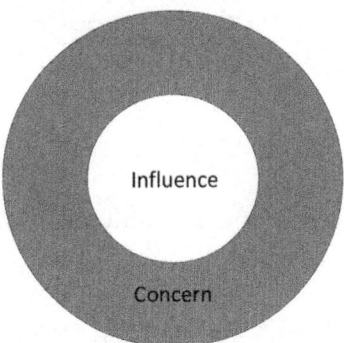

Figure 15: Circle of Influence

Reinhold Niebuhr reflects the intelligence of this approach in the words of the Serenity Prayer:

"Grant me the courage to change the things I can, the serenity to accept the things I can't, and the wisdom to know the difference."

When you help the mentee recognise what they can control and what they can't, it immediately reduces stress. You can empower them to focus their energy and effort where it will make most difference. You will help them take responsibility and plan actions.

Build a Learning Mindset

Mentors want to help mentees become strong, resilient and capable because we know that the future holds challenges and change.

Dr Carol Dweck and her team at Harvard researched students' attitudes about failure. They identified an important reason that some are devastated while others bounce back. It's mindset.

A fixed mindset represents a belief that intelligence and ability are set and unchanging, whereas someone with a growth mindset acknowledges that people can learn, become more skilled, and that time and effort help them improve.

The growth mindset is consistent with the concept of brain plasticity that means that brains change in response to experience. Neural growth is increased through using good strategies, practice and asking questions. Furthermore, if you believe your brain can grow you behave differently.

Foster a growth mindset by sharing these ideas:

- Effort and perseverance can lead to improvement
- Challenges are opportunities to develop
- Mistakes are valuable learning experiences
- Feedback is useful

Focus on Talents and Strengths

We are each born with our own personality—patterns of thinking feeling and behaving. These are further shaped by our environment —the people, emotional and physical surroundings. This combination, often referred to as nature and nurture, shapes our unique characteristics and abilities. Included in this package are our natural talents. Some of these will be nurtured and become strengths. Others remain in potential, awaiting the opportunity to be developed. Most people have far more potential than they realise. Talents may remain dormant, out of awareness or unrecognised, but they are there, and remain throughout life.

Everyone has strengths and weaknesses, and while effort and perseverance can improve performance where we lack skill, decades of research show that working hard in areas we lack talent is not nearly as productive as developing talents and building on strengths.

The work of the late Donald Clifton examined the question "What if, instead of looking at what's wrong with people we focused on what's right?" The global research organisation Gallup has continued to explore what is possible when people develop talents and strengths. Many organisations are now teaching individuals and teams how to identify and build strengths because there is direct link between using strengths and bottom line results. The CliftonStrengths Assessment is a reliable and valid instrument that is widely used for this purpose. Certified strengths coaches are available in most parts of the world.

Even without the use of an instrument, your conversations can highlight their existing strengths and talents. You can help your mentee discover and build on what they are best at.

There are other ways to recognise talents because natural born temperament is like a magnet that pulls us to develop the raw ingredients nature provided.

Look for evidence of:

- **Magnetic attraction:** a sense of a "calling" to a vocation, yearning to do particular things, a strong inclination toward some aspects of their job.
- **Rapid Learning:** a knack for doing certain things. Quickly picking up techniques, where it's easy and enjoyable to learn because they are very interested and can't get enough of the topic.
- **Instinctive Response:** Things they naturally do well. Perhaps they are a strategic thinker, a people person, a good influencer, or they just get things done.
- **Immense Satisfaction:** certain aspects of their work thrills them, perhaps it's solving problems, organising events, negotiating a great deal or helping others grow. It's their thing. Watch them light up, become energised when they talk about certain topics. It's a major clue that this is an area of natural talent.

Getting the mentee to talk about their accomplishments, past events, hobbies, and activities they enjoy and are good at is a very good way to identify talents and strengths.

There is a formula used for job interviews that is very helpful for structuring anecdotes about achievements. It's called the STAR technique where you ask the mentee to outline the situation and/or task, describe the actions they took, then talk about the results. If the mentee is preparing for an interview, it's useful for them to practice creating succinct and relevant STAR stories. If not, it's still very helpful to use it to explore their past and draw out talents and strength that they may not recognise.

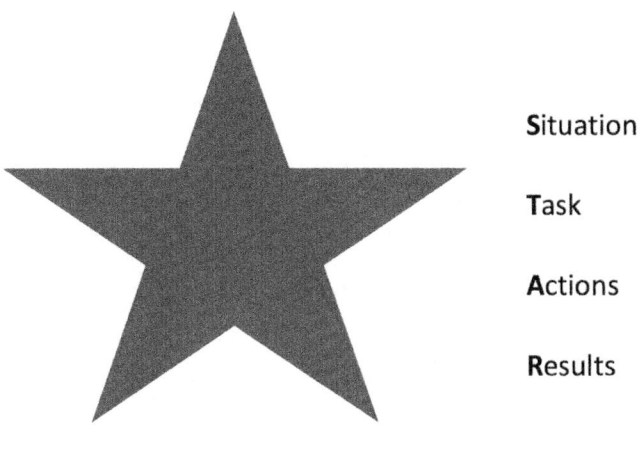

Figure 16: STAR

"Tell me about a time when you ..."

"How did you accomplish that?"

"What specifically did you do that helped?"

"What happened as a result?"

You want to elicit as much as possible from the mentee and some people are modest, not used to talking about their achievements, or unaware of the value of what they've done. So use probing questions with your respectful curiosity to draw them out.

"Tell me more about that"

"What else?"

"How did you work that out?"

"What was the biggest challenge?"

"How did you approach that?"

"What abilities helped you do that?"

Your job is firstly, to unpick these anecdotes to highlight how they demonstrate the use of the mentee's talents and strengths. Then, having identified them in a particular example, look for illustration of use in other situations. Assist your mentee to become aware of themes and patterns of behaviour that are evidence of natural talent.

Your aim is to help them see their strengths. My experience is that people often are blind to some of their abilities. They take for granted natural talents because they are skills that come easily to them. You'll hear them say things like: "Oh, anyone could do that," unaware that a particular ability is not universal.

Once the mentee becomes aware of talents and strengths you can discuss ways they can develop, use, and enjoy them. Teach them how to describe them for personal satisfaction, in resumes and job interviews. Make sure they know how strengths can be applied in work, and how they contribute in various roles.

4
RESILIENCE

Resilience is the ability to bounce back after some sort of setback—from the minor and relatively trivial things that happen day-to-day, to major, life-changing or traumatic events. Our ability to deal with and recover from life's inevitable challenges affects our health and well-being, our work and enjoyment and quality of life. With what we've all been through the last few years, we need to build resilience - our own as well as others.

Petrea King, CEO of The Quest For Life Foundation, talks about "Life's Ds": Diagnosis, a life-threatening illness or major injury, divorce, death of a loved one, depression and disaster. Every one of us has or will face one or more of these ourselves or with someone very close to us. And when we do, it affects every area of our life.

Then there's stress at work. As well as the personal toll it takes on people, workplace stress costs organisations and the economy, dearly.

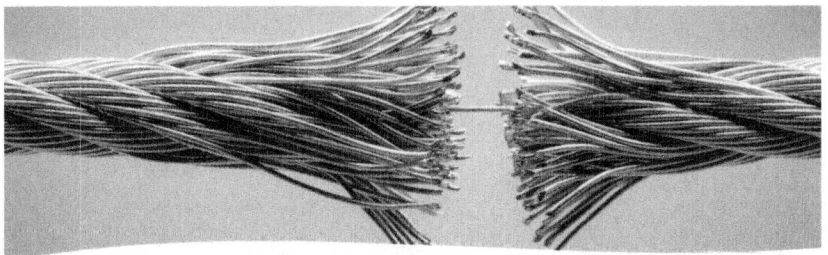

Workplace stress is costing the Australian economy **$14.8 billion a year**

Stress-related presenteeism and absenteeism are directly costing Australian employers **$10.11 billion a year**

3.2 days per worker Are lost each year through workplace stress

Figure 17: Workplace Stress. *Source: Medibank Private (2008) The Cost of Workplace Stress in Australia*

We can't avoid challenges in life or at work, indeed we don't want to. According to the Yerks-Dodson Law for peak performance, there is an optimal and constructive level of stress. Too much and we burn out; too little and we rust out!

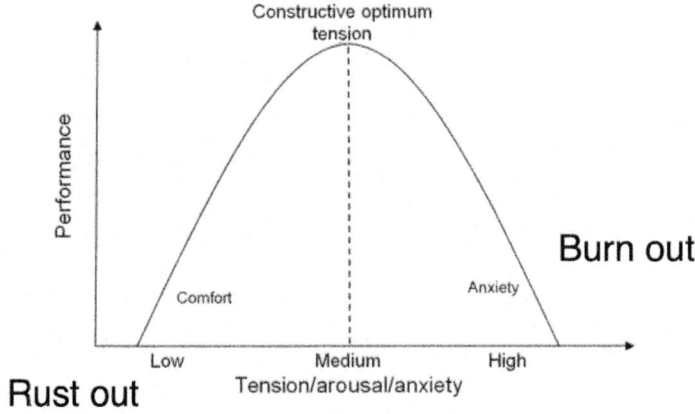

Figure 18: Yerks-Dodson Law

In the workplace, we need to find the "Goldilocks" level where tasks that are not beyond our capabilities because that causes anxiety; but are not below our capabilities because that causes boredom.

Kids are born adventurers, but if they don't get that "Goldilocks" balance of risk and safety, they can't build resilience. There has been a disturbing trend in parenting that is seeing some young people in the workplace now, with low levels of resilience because they haven't had the benefit of the right level of challenges, disappointments, and obstacles. For some there's been a shift from Helicopter parenting—where parents hover over their kids, trying to see them safe to "Lawnmower" parenting—where parents actively smooth out all obstacles so kids never experience rough ground or challenges. This does not prepare them for the realities of life or work. Wrapping kids in cotton wool doesn't protect them in the long-run. We can build our resilience "muscles" at any time, but the earlier the better. Although youthful adventure can go horribly wrong.

In 2018, an adventurous junior soccer team explored a cave near their home, a remote Thai town, Mai Sae. Monsoon rains came early, and the 12 boys aged 11-17 and their coach became trapped in a cavern they'd reached via 2 kilometres of twisting, narrow and now mostly submerged tunnels.

Against all odds, Thai Navy SEAL divers supported by international, expert cave divers saved them after 9 days.

Joint Australians of the Year Richard "Harry" Harris, an Australian anaesthetist and retired vet Craig Challen, both expert cave divers, were part of the rescue team. In a feat never before attempted, Harry anaesthetised each boy to prevent panic as divers swam them out with face masks, wet suits and oxygen tanks. Craig Challen was in the first of several larger unflooded chambers along the way and checked each boy's vital signs and helped get them to the next underwater stage. In what some described as a miracle, they saved all the boys and their coach, though one Thai Navy SEAL died in the attempt. Rescuers were all hailed as heroes and awarded bravery medals.

Despite the misadventure of the Thai boys, Dr. Harris used his platform to encourage kids to get outdoors and find their inner explorer. "Maybe get a few grazed knees and stub their toes. Climb a tree, get off their screens and get outside". There's a balance for kids between risk and safety and the same is true for adults.

In the workplace, there are times to speak up and be bold and times to hold your tongue. For example, do you call out racist, sexist, ignorant or cruel comments and behaviour?

Likewise, with decision-making, if you are too risk-averse, you make no decisions, or become bogged down in analysis-paralysis. Yet too much risk-taking can be dangerous and reckless.

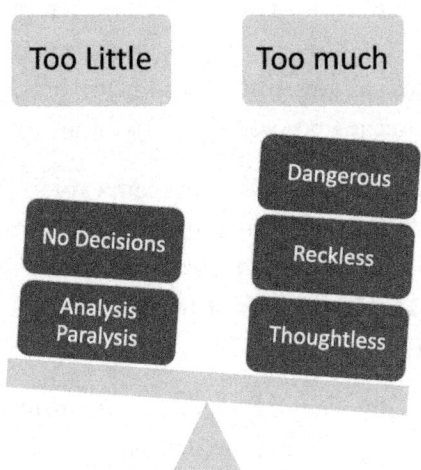

Figure 19: Risk

Our approach to risk is not just a question of courage. It involves consideration of consequences. As a mentor, you can help your mentee figure out potential consequences of any action and whether potential benefits outweigh possible negatives.

Experience allows us to develop risk tolerance. If we have coped with adversity and got through some tough times, we may meet new challenges, feeling more confident that we can deal with them. Sometimes, a conversation with a mentor reminds us of that.

"When have you faced a challenge before?"

"What helped you get through that?"

"How could you apply those tactics in this situation?"

There are some situations where you are more risk-averse than others. For example, I am financially risk-averse. I figure that at nearly seventy years of age I have less time and ability to recover from any mistakes managing my money.

Typical challenges in the workplace include:

- Change—mergers, new boss, new job, redundancies
- Bullying, racism, sexism, bias, discrimination
- Poor management
- Team-members who don't pull their weight
- Technology

Changes are not always bad, often they are good, but they can present a challenge as we adjust, particularly when we haven't chosen the change.

When we find ourselves in challenging circumstances, we need:

- **Coping skills:** ways to survive the immediate threat
- **Self-management skills:** things we can do to prevent or reduce risk, and
- **Influencing skills:** steps we take to shape a positive future

Figure 20: Resilience

When we feel threatened, we instantly react. Whether a threat is real or imagined, physical or emotional, the brain triggers the Fight/Flight/Freeze response that affects every aspect of our body.

The brain works differently in fight/flight/freeze mode. We hear, see, and process everything in the context of survival. That means we fight back, run away or, like a deer in the headlights, freeze, unable to say or do anything.

We have all experienced threat that triggers the brain's defence systems at work and in life. Perhaps in a relatively small way, such as a hurtful comment or more harmful bullying, racism or sexism, bias or discrimination.

Sometimes we fight, sometimes we flee, sometimes we do nothing. Sometimes one of these is useful for coping in the moment and sometimes not.

Coping skills allow us to react to a threat in the best way we can. You can't bounce back if you can't survive. The following is a real-life example, but it provides a metaphor for less life-threatening events you can apply this to workplace situations.

During the 2018 Australian Black Summer bushfire season, there was quite confronting advertising telling us we should decide when to leave our property, should it be threatened. People die when they leave it too late. They try to defend their home in the face of a catastrophic fire. They are operating in fight mode when they should flee. The way to react to a life-threatening situation that is impossible to control is to leave as fast as possible.

The bushfire advertising made us proactively plan ahead, decide early, before being caught in the moment. Yes, we can clear combustible materials from around our home, put out spot fires caused by embers ahead of the fire-front, but we must get out before it becomes impossible to do so and we must know when that is. All emergency responders have safety protocols drummed into them. They train, they practice and we have to do the same.

After Black Saturday, survivors, emergency services and government worked together. Each used their influence to use lessons learned to create a safer environment.

Given the high cost of workplace stress, it's no surprise that organisations are introducing proactive and creative strategies to improve workplaces.

How to Build Resilience

Dr Sam Harvey, a psychiatrist with the Black Dog Institute, says that: Building resilience is one way we can all reduce our stress at work and contribute to a more mentally healthy workplace.

Resilience isn't something you either have or you don't.

It's not a magical quality, it's not a trait.

Resilience is a combination of thinking, actions and behaviours and, just like building muscle strength, mental strength requires work to develop. There are ways you can build resilience through your thinking, actions, and behaviour. We need to work to build resilience muscles—the thinking, actions and behaviours that strengthen us.

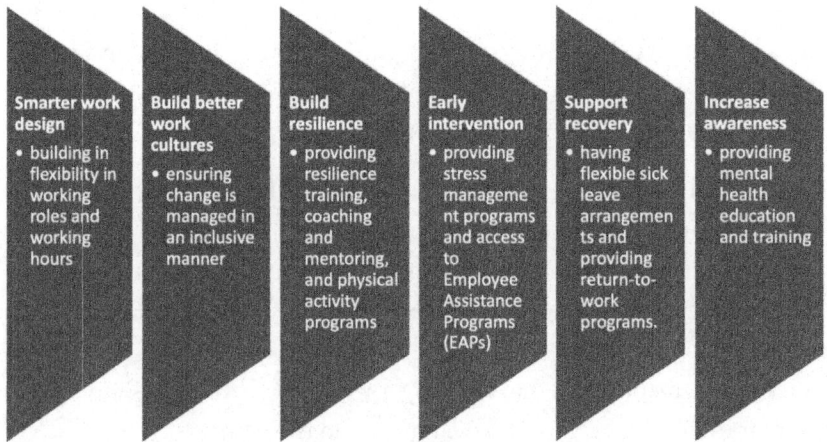

Figure 21: Ways to Improve Mental Health in the Workplace (sources: *Dr Sam Harvey, Black Dog Institute and UNSW*)

Fight/flight/freeze is very much an instinctive stimulus-response reaction to threat. Stress is the same - something in the environment triggers an automatic reaction, but by building resilience, we put a gap or a buffer between stimulus and response. We expand our circle of influence; we have more control.

We can start with our thinking.

Resilience Thinking

This means choosing thoughts that serve us better, using in-the-moment coping thinking strategies.

You need to be proactive, plan and practice these so that they become your default in times of challenge.

Advanced Mentoring Skills

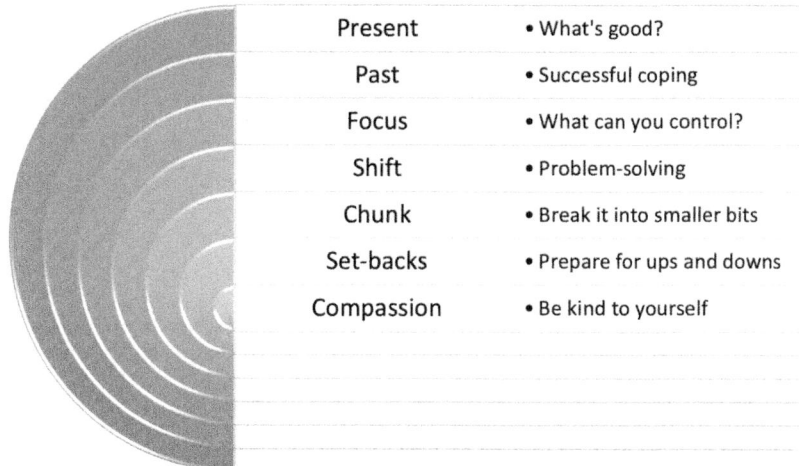

Figure 22: Resilience Thinking

When you are feeling overwhelm, can you be present and look for what is good? What's going well?

It often helps to look to the past and remind yourself of things you've coped with previously. Think of the skills and strengths that got you through.

Remembering the circle of concern and circle of influence (see Chapter 3), focus on what you can control, maybe taking slow, deep breaths (fight/flight, anxiety or panic can trigger rapid, shallow breathing).

Shift your thinking towards problem solving. What's the outcome you want? What's in the way? What can you do differently to progress?

Chunk big problems into smaller pieces that are easier to manage.

Sometimes we fall into all-or-nothing thinking. Our way is blocked, so we're doomed to failure. Try to think of these blocks as setbacks, not insurmountable obstacles. We all have difficulties, life is seldom all smooth sailing.

Learn to be kind to yourself, have compassion. Are you your harshest critic? Check your self-talk, those things you say to yourself, the little insults, self-inflicted put-downs, the doubts, the imposter syndrome. You wouldn't be that unkind to someone else, so don't do it to yourself!

Resilience Actions

Figure 23: Resilience Actions

Connect. We know that survivors have good social connections so nourish your vital relationships—make time for coffee, phone calls and other catch-ups. Don't constantly put socialising off because you're too busy.

Reach out to your network—when you're in trouble people say: "let me know if there's anything I can do." Do. Ask. Most people mean it when they offer help, but they don't know what you need. You may have to be explicit: "I just need to blow off steam," "I need a shoulder to cry on," "I need someone to listen and not give advice." Etc.

Talk to people—don't hold it all in or you're likely to explode. Choose friends or colleagues you can trust and confide in. If there is no one you feel confident in, or the matter is too serious, find a professional.

Use your organisation's Employee Assistance Scheme or ask your GP for a referral. You don't have to go it alone.

Self-nurturing is proactive. You do this to build resilience. I learned about self-nurturing from a rape counsellor, who watched so many of her good-hearted professional colleagues burn out. She had a whole suite of things that nurtured her physical, mental, emotional and spiritual wellbeing.

Choose what works for you, be it meditation, yoga, running, art, massage, hobbies, whatever relaxes you, strengthens you and brings you pleasure or respite, then build it into your life, every day if you can but certainly every week. It's not an indulgence to look after yourself, it's a necessity.

Set realistic goals and celebrate achievements. At the end of every day, review what you've accomplished. A simple to do list with items ticked off is enough. As long as you complete the most important ones, you can take satisfaction from it.

Focus on strengths. Your best results will come from building on your strengths. Identify your natural talents with an instrument like the Clifton StrengthsFinder and develop them. Manage your weaknesses.

We all need a sense of purpose. Find the meaning in your work. How does it help others, make the world better, contribute to something you care about or align with your values?

If you're not doing something you love in your job, make sure you do in your own time as a volunteer, as a hobby or with the people you love.

Is there a cause you believe in? Can you contribute to something you feel is worthwhile? Do you have a personal purpose for your life?

Resilience Behaviours

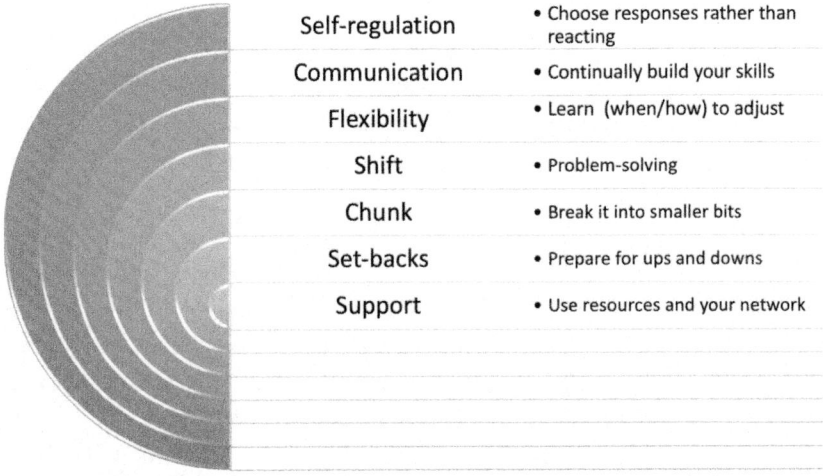

Figure 24: Resilience Behaviours

Awareness is often called emotional intelligence. It involves noticing your own reactions, creating that gap between stimulus and response and self-regulation, choosing how you respond rather than automatically reacting. Emotional intelligence also considers other people's emotional reactions. If you can see that someone is in fight/flight/freeze, you know that emotion, not rational thinking, is driving their behaviour. Is there some way you can reduce the threat they feel?

Listening often lessens fight/flight/freeze reactions—your own and those of others. Suspend judgment, we tend to classify everything as right/wrong, good/bad, but we don't have to jump to those conclusions. When we build resilience muscles, we are strong enough to pause and choose to understand their point of view. We don't have to agree or disagree.

Assertiveness means speaking up, calmly standing up for your rights —not aggressively trampling over the rights of others—but stating what you want. It takes some skill and courage and practice. It's not always appropriate to assert your rights and you must make an intelligent choice.

This is where flexibility comes in. You decide when and how to adjust, perhaps accommodate someone else's needs. When to stand your ground, when to back down and when to leave.

We all need resilience and we always do the best we can at the time. When we know better we can do better.

PART II
CRITICAL SKILLS FOR MENTORS

5

TRUST

Every relationship depends on trust. It doesn't matter whether it is spouses or colleagues, a family or a team, the level of trust strongly influences success.

Trust in the workplace has been shown to increase:

- Productivity
- Energy
- Collaboration
- Retention
- Performance

And, trust reduces chronic stress

So, are there skills and behaviours that will build trust? You bet!

Paul Zack is the founding director of the Center for Neuroeconomics Studies, professor of economics, psychology and management at Claremont Graduate University and author of *Trust Factor: The Science of Creating High Performance Companies*. Here's what he found in scientific studies comparing high trust and low trust in organisations over 10 years:

- 74% less stress
- 106% more energy at work
- 50% higher productivity
- 13% fewer sick days
- 76% more engagement
- 29% more satisfaction with life
- 40% less burnout
- 50% more loyal—plan to stay with their employer
- 88% would recommend as place to work
- enjoy job 60% more
- 11% more empathy with colleagues
- 41% more sense of accomplishment
- earn 17% more

Source: Paul J. Zack (2017) The Neuro Science of Trust. Harvard Business Review. Jan-Feb Issue 2017.

The Roy Morgan organisation surveys Australians' level of trust in various professions each year using ethics and honesty as the rating. Nurses have topped the list for the last 23 years.

Advanced Mentoring Skills

94% Nurses	50% Accountants	17% Union Leaders
89% Doctors	37% Public Servants	17% TV Reporters
84% Pharmacists	35% Lawyers	16% Federal MPs
81% School Teachers	34% Public Opinion Pollsters	16% State MPs
80% Engineer	34% Ministers of Religion	14% Talk-back Radio Announcers
79% Dentists	33% Bank Managers	11% Stockbrokers
76% Police	25% Directors of Public Companies	10% Insurance Brokers
74% High Court Judges	25% Financial Planners	7% Real Estate Agents
71% State Supreme Court Judges	20% Newspaper Journalists	5% Advertising People
66% University Lecturers	18% Business Executives	4% Car Salesmen

Figure 25:*Percentage of Australians rating the professions as "Very High" or High" for ethics and honesty (Source: Roy Morgan 2017)*

What is Trust?

What is it that allows us to trust someone?

I believe there is a trust zone that is a culmination of several elements: credibility, reliability, mutuality and reciprocity.

Some of what opens our trust zone is emotional, and some are rational.

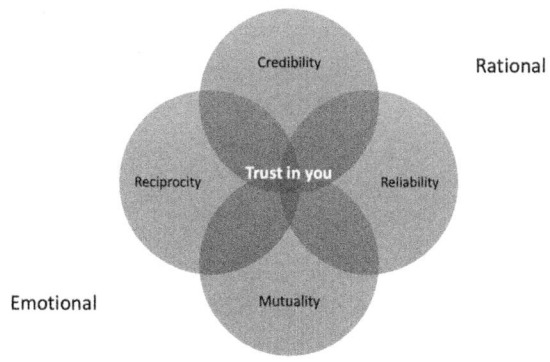

Figure 26: Trust

Those we consider trustworthy typically share some characteristics that allow them to establish **credibility** with us. We believe in their:

- **Integrity**—they are honest and congruent. They do not lie. Their words and deeds match, they "walk the talk". They act in alignment with the values they espouse.
- **Capability**—they have knowledge, skills, abilities that inspire our confidence. They know what they are talking about, their information is reliable. They have experience in their field.

We consider them **reliable**:

- **Performance**—they produce results. Get things done. Do the things that make for effectiveness. It is not enough to look good, they must fulfil the promise, meet expectations.
- **Consistency**. They turn up, meet commitments, do what they say they will, on time.

With people we trust, there is a sense of **mutuality.**

- **Intent**—they are positive toward us. They care about us, not just themselves, and will act in our best interests, not purely self-interest.
- **Motivation**—they are straight-forward and their reasons are transparent. There is no hidden agenda

Interestingly, you are more likely to get trust if you give trust. It is **reciprocated** when you show:

- **Respect**—you acknowledge the person, their intelligence and autonomy and their right to be treated as an adult
- **Confidence**—you show faith in their ability and believe they will do my part

Trust-Building Skills

So trust is not something you have or you don't. There are behaviours and skills that you can develop.

1. Communication—listening, questioning, non-verbal cues
2. Feedback—positive and genuine and, once you establish trust, corrective feedback
3. Self-disclosure—to help them get to know you as a person

Listening, questioning and feedback are the subject of their own chapters in this book.

Self-disclosure needs to be appropriate and build your credibility in their eyes. You want to let them get to know you enough to trust you and see that you have some experience or expertise relevant to their needs.

The Johari Window, developed by Joseph Luft and Harry Ingham, is a classic model that shows the potential for growth by expanding openness in a relationship.

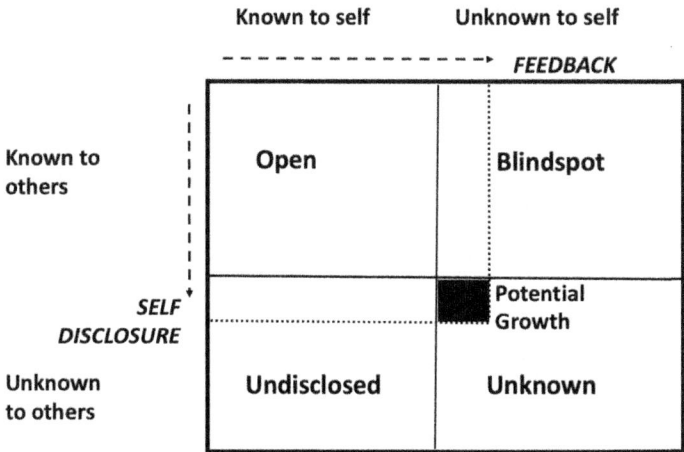

Figure 27: *Johari Window (Source: Joseph Luft and Harry Ingham)*

The open window pane—what we and they know—grows through feedback to them and self-disclosure. However, people instinctively know that when you give someone information about yourself, you are also giving them power over you. Others may disapprove, dispute or even condemn or ridicule the opinions, beliefs or behaviours you divulge.

Fear of judgement causes people to be defensive. This is a barrier to all communication, but it especially blocks self-disclosure. Your challenge as a mentor is to create a relationship where people can express themselves without fear of being judged.

To build the self-confidence necessary for self-disclosure, mentors can help mentees to:

- Find examples of success in the past. This could include obstacles they have overcome, problems resolved or difficult situations that they have got through;
- Make a list of positive achievements, review and add to it often; then
- Set appropriate and achievable new goals.

This process enables incremental and realistic expansion of the mentee's self-image as an achiever.

As well as building the mentee's self-confidence, mentors need to gain their trust and confidence.

Stephen Covey describes the "emotional bank account" as a metaphor for the amount of trust in a relationship. You make deposits and withdrawals with your words and actions. Listening with acceptance, seeking to understand fully and appreciate what the mentee has to say and why they are saying it is the single biggest way to improve their trust and confidence in you.

Mentoring conversations focus on intentions and outcomes. This means talking about what the mentee wants and why it is important to them. Sometimes mentees don't know what they want or have difficulty articulating it. So mentors have to dig deeper to draw them out. This calls for patient and careful listening and sensitive questioning. Asking anyone "why" they want something tends to result in defensive justification or arguments that entrench their ideas more firmly.

Encourage Self-disclosure

Here are sample questions that encourage self-disclosure when used with accepting tone and body language (you can prepare questions in your own words).

"If you had that, what would it do for you?"

"Can you say some more about why that's important to you?"

"What is it about that you would enjoy?"

"How do you think that would feel?"

"Imagine you have achieved that. What do you see?"

"What will change for you when you do that?"

When people feel safe and accepted, they will take the risk of self-disclosure and open to the possibility of setting and achieving their goals. This can inspire a spiral of success that mentors foster and build.

Trust is a product of both rational and emotional processes that take place in the brain. Emotional reactions are fast and triggered in the limbic area of the brain at the base of the skull. Rational thinking takes longer and happens in the neocortex, just behind your forehead.

It is the instantaneous emotional reaction of the brain that triggers the fight/flight/freeze reaction. We evolved from ancient ancestors whose survival depended on their ability to react fast to any threat by defending themselves, running away or hiding.

Your evolved brain is constantly vigilant, scanning the environment 5 times per second for potential threats. In every interaction with other people, your brain is asking: "can I trust or must I defend?" When there is trust, relationships are built and conversations are productive, but it's surprisingly easy to trigger defensiveness—just a look, a tone of voice or a word can do it.

The brain can't tell the difference between a genuine threat and an imagined one. You know this if you've ever watched a scary movie and felt your heart thumping or nearly jumped out of your seat when the on-screen raptor leaped at you. And, once fight/flight/freeze has been primed, you stay jumpy for some time. Think of the implications of feeling threatened in the workplace! Hopefully, people don't come out swinging, but emotionally and physically, that's what their brain and body are gearing up for. This is why we sometimes see aggressive-defensive behaviours or passive-defensive behaviours at work. Start noticing aggressive and passive-defensive actions. Keep in mind both are actually defensive behaviours.

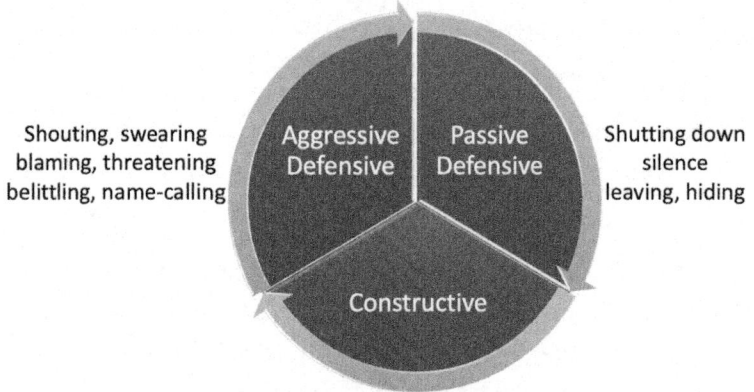

Figure 28: Aggressive/Passive/Constructive

As mentors, we want to encourage constructive behaviours and the less people feel defensive, the better. Here is where knowing a little neuroscience can help.

Social Drivers: Levers of Threat and Reward

When they describe how the brain seeks safety for us, neuroscientists talk about 5 social drivers that create threat/reward.

We can think of these as levers. When the lever is in the toward position, the brain perceives reward and safety and responds with trust.

Flick the lever the other way and the message is threat, defences are triggered.

Dr Norman Chorn and Dr. Terri Hunter use the acronym SAFETY to help us remember the 5 levers, plus your preferred or dominant driver.

- Security—certainty, predictability, stability
- Autonomy—freedom to decide and choose
- Fairness—equity, transparency, social justice
- Esteem—status in relation to others, recognition
- Trust—belonging to a group or tribe, feeling safe in relationships with others
- Your dominant driver — all the levers will move you, but one tends to hold more sway

As you read the next few pages, see if you can identify which social driver means most to you.

Security

We use routines, habits, and the rules of thumb to make millions of minor decisions each day. These default settings allow us to do things without thinking. It's as if the brain is on auto-pilot. This frees up the executive function to deal with immediate and important cognitive tasks.

The brain hates disruption and the unexpected. Because switching off auto-pilot to use the executive brain to process the new data and act deliberately instead of out of habit requires effort uses vital energy.

Security to the brain means routine, ordinary, no surprises. So, ambiguity, confusion, or unmet expectations are experienced as a threat and incite defensiveness; whereas familiarity, previous or similar experience, clear expectations, being prepared, forewarned or briefed about expectations signal safety.

Autonomy

Adults want to be self-directing. Most of us hate rigid rules, being given orders or micromanaged. We resent top-down planning that robs us of input and feels disempowering. Our brain perceives these as threats.

Reward is the satisfying feeling that we are in control, are independent and have choices, we can work in collaboration.

Fairness

What will flick this lever into threat is unfair treatment, injustice, the perception of favouritism, preferential treatment, or arbitrary decisions. Reward is experienced when there is transparency, a logical rationale for decisions and equity.

Esteem

We instinctively understand the importance of status. High-status individuals get more. Whether it's food, money, sex, the corner office, the car or parking spot or better assignments at work.

The brain is constantly evaluating our status in relation to others. Feeling judged or looked down on, negative feedback, not winning in a competitive situation, lack of money or having to do the dirty work all can lower self-esteem and raise defensiveness. Mastery—self-efficacy, seeing ourselves as competent, being treated with respect, being acknowledged, positive feedback and praise are rewarding.

Trust

Rejection, isolation, loneliness, feeling different and socially disconnected are very threatening and causes great pain. The brain experiences social pain in the same way as physical pain. Trust, in this context, means we feel safe. Inclusion, rapport, empathy and friendship are rewards that bring us closer to each other.

Your Dominant Social Driver

All five social drivers are important, but usually one is more dominant than others for each of us. That means that it is easier to trigger brain response—trust or defend—in this area. Your dominant driver will filter your perception of others and events.

When interacting with people, you will be inclined to use your dominant driver, but if they have a different one, yours has less appeal to them and it's harder to build the relationship. So you'll need to cover all 5 unless you know their preferred driver and can "speak their language".

In mentoring, you build **security** by:

- Agreeing ground rules
- Discussing expectations
- Sharing an agenda prior to meeting

As a mentor, you preserve the mentee's **autonomy** by:

- Listening more than you speak and asking more than telling
- Encouraging them to make their own decisions
- Discussing their intentions, actions and likely outcomes so that they can take responsibility

As a mentor, you can show **fairness** through:

- An open mind that sees both sides of an argument
- Describing situations from different perspectives
- Championing equity

As a mentor, maintain the mentee's **esteem** through:

- Treating them as a colleague, an equal, not patronising them
- Being slow to give advice, even when asked—facilitate their thinking and decision-making, instead
- Providing positive feedback and/or getting them to reflect and recall their own success

As a mentor, develop **trust** by:

- Building rapport with the mentee every time you speak to re-establish the relationship
- Reminding them that conversations are confidential and keeping their confidences
- Being willing to disclose (appropriate) information about yourself to show you trust them

6

ADVANCED LISTENING

The gift of mentoring is listening to a mentee in ways few people experience in life, unless they consult a trained counsellor or coach.

We may hear easily enough, but true listening can be hard. It doesn't come naturally to most. It involves skills that are developed.

A lot of listening is superficial and shallow, involving little genuine effort. Poor listening can cause misunderstandings and mistakes. It results in preventable problems and faulty judgment. In business, as in relationships, the cost of poor listening is high.

Passive listening is lazy. Mentoring is active and listening is a focused use of skills. It's difficult – until you have practiced and practiced, so it becomes second nature.

Listening well is good for you. It doesn't just improve communication, it's one key to building resilience and maintaining balance in your life. It boosts positive emotions, which are a key component of happiness and, listening affects your learning, your attention, your interpersonal relationships, your ability to regulate stress, and your ability to sleep.

Listening is important in all relationships. As mentors, it's especially important that we show a willingness to be present and really hear our mentees. We invite them to confide in us, because we have committed to a helpful relationship. Whether it's focused on career development, supporting them through challenges, or accelerating their growth and potential.

In mentoring, the purpose of listening is to elicit what mentees have to say. We want to bring to the surface their thoughts and feelings, values and priorities and increase their ability to generate insight from their own experience so that they can navigate a way forward. The type of listening required is one where we open ourselves to receive—we seek to understand the person and their perspective—from what they say.

What Gets in the Way?

One major problem is that brain capacity for listening far exceeds the capacity of speech. Typically, we can speak at 125-175 words per minute, while the brain can process 400 wpm. No matter how fast someone speaks, the brain has excess capacity. What does the brain do with its excess capacity? Anything it wants!

If you're like most people, you find yourself thinking about what you'll have for lunch, whether you'll be late for your next meeting, or that email you haven't yet answered, even when you have committed to listen.

If you meditate, you know how the mind seems to have a mind of its own! Though you are trying to focus on nothing but your breath, or an image or mantra, your mind will take you off down a rabbit hole any time it gets a chance. I recommend meditation practice to improve your overall wellbeing and ability to listen.

Another problem is that ears never close, unlike our ability to rest our eyes by closing them, we have no "ear lids". Ears are always open, they work even when we're sleeping. Millions of bits of information are flooding all our senses all the time. Filters protect us from overload, but sometimes filters work too well!

Quick Quiz

Rate yourself on each of the items below. Only you will see the result so you can be as honest as your self-awareness allows.

The rating scale is: 0 = Never, 1 = Sometimes, 2 = Often, 3 = Always

When I listen, I find myself:

1. Easily distracted
2. Faking attention, acting polite
3. Reacting to emotional words
4. Interrupting frequently
5. Tuning out on uninteresting topics
6. Daydreaming if the speaker is slow
7. Jumping to conclusions
8. Finding fault with the message
9. Thinking of what I want to say

Adapted from Eastwood Atwater (1981) I Hear You. Prentice Hall.

So how did you go? The highest score is 27, the lowest zero, but I think if any of us got that we're kidding ourselves. Obviously, the lower the score the better, but what I want you to do with this is to identify what you're worst at, because that gives you a goal to work towards improving. What is the most important area for you to improve?

What Does it Take to Hear?

> "Most people do not listen with the intent to understand, they listen with the intent to reply."
>
> — STEPHEN COVEY

In his classic, *7 Habits of Highly Effective People*, one habit is "Seek first to understand, then be understood." This is a fantastic principle for mentors to adopt. If you really want to influence people, whether it is by imparting your wisdom or challenging their thinking, you need to understand them first. Covey describes 5 levels of listening. At levels 1–4, we are hearing from our own perspective, focused on ourselves, limiting our understanding of the other person. But at level 5 we exercise empathy, understanding their perspective.

Level: Ignoring, whether deliberate or inadvertent, we've all experienced it. You feel rejected, frustrated, and sad. Neurological responses trigger defensiveness—the fight/flight/freeze described in the previous chapter on trust. If preoccupied, you might find yourself ignoring others, not listening.

Level 2: Pretend listening, going through the motions, nodding, saying, "OK", "I see". This happens when you're distracted, or feel you need to be polite, but are really not interested.

Level 3: Selective listening, paying attention to only parts of what is being said, easily slipping back into pretend listening, interrupting, or being impatient for people to get to the point.

Level 4: Attentive listening—giving time and attention. This is good but, it sometimes falls short of real understanding. Level 4 attentive listening may still involve:

- Evaluating—judging based on your values, priorities and needs

- Advising—recommending from your point of view
- Probing—for information you think is important
- Interpreting—what's happening as you see it

Level 5: Empathic Listening—trying to see the world as they see it. Not projecting your own interpretation. Suspending any judgment. Listening with ears for not only words and meaning, but also tone and vocal emphasis. You listen with your eyes to pick up non-verbal messages. You listen with your heart to tune into their feelings and you allow your intuition to get a sense of the unspoken. You can use active listening skills and reflection to allow them to confirm or clarify what you sense is what they want to express.

Empathy differs from sympathy. Sympathy is when *you have the same feelings* as the other person. Empathy is *understanding what they are feeling.*

As a mentor, listening well begins with setting a firm intention. What we aim for is level 5 empathic listening, because at level 4 we're still in our own frame of reference, whereas in level empathic listening we step into the mentee's world.

Five Techniques for Better Listening

If you want to be a better listener, develop these habits:

1. **Silence**—don't interrupt, don't jump in with your own story, opinions or advice. Let them speak.
2. **Focus on them**—attend to what they are saying and what they are not saying. You want to understand what they mean and that doesn't always come out in the first words they say. Notice their non-verbal communication. Suspend your judgment and listen to their point of view. Try to pick up their values and priorities, needs and wants.
3. **Minimal response**—you need to show them you are fully present and listening without interrupting their flow. So give

positive non-verbal signs of listening. Keep your verbal responses short ("mm-hm", "I see", "tell me more") to encourage them to say more.

4. **Reflect**—when it is your turn to speak, resist the urge to give advice! Instead, reflect to the mentee what they have said, emphasising their feelings. Don't parrot their words instead, paraphrase, summarise, or restate using some of their words and some of your own.

5. **Ask good questions**—when you reflect, the mentee will confirm or clarify their thoughts. Sometimes, that is all they need. People often want to ventilate or express themselves. They're not seeking a solution from you! Even when they do want an answer, the opportunity to think out loud and being heard is enough for them to come up with their own solution. If you do need to take the conversation further, do so with open questions, asked with respectful curiosity. And continue listening!

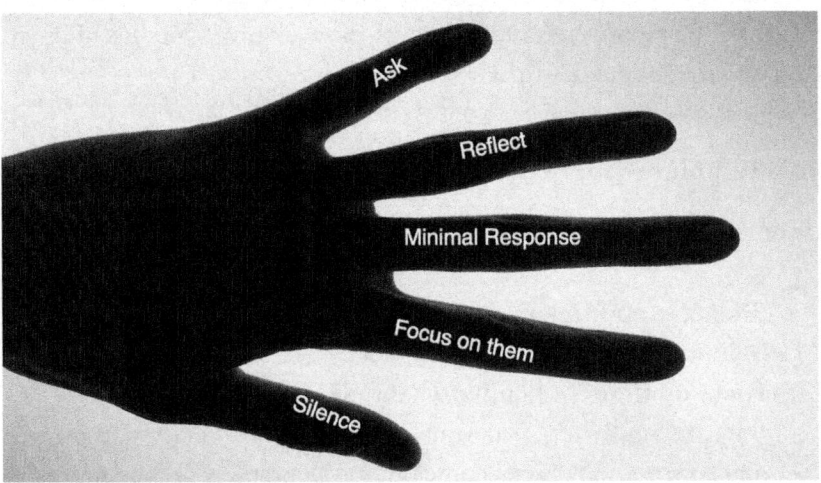

Figure 29: Hand Model

The activity below gives you a handy tool to remember the 5 techniques for better listening during a mentoring conversation. First, draw an outline of your hand on paper and label each finger as shown above.

1. Silence

Close your fingers with your thumb sticking out as if you were giving the thumbs up. Touch your thumb to your chin and as you do, say to yourself "silence". Do that again 3 times—touch your thumb to your chin and say "silence". This will be a reminder that the first step in really understanding what someone is saying is to keep quiet.

In fact, with your thumb on your chin, it's quite easy to lift your pointer finger to your lips, a further reminder to yourself to shhh.

2. Focus on Them

Next, keeping your pointer finger extended, pivot your hand away from you toward an imaginary mentee and say to yourself, "focus on them". Bring your hand back to the previous "shh" position and pivot back and forth 3 more times, repeating "focus on them".

3. Minimal Response

Relax the pointer finger now and gently apply a small amount of pressure with your middle finger to the fleshy area beneath the thumb. Look at the caption on the middle finger in the diagram. Repeat that now three times as you gently press that area with your middle finger. "Minimal response, minimal response, minimal response".

4. Reflect

Now try to move your ring finger, just a little. Imaging you have a beautiful, sparkling diamond ring and it reminds you to reflect. Repeat to yourself "reflect, reflect, reflect".

5. Ask

Finally, raise your little finger. You've listened well and to go deeper, you need to ask. Remember, these are open questions, with respectful curiosity. Raise the little finger and repeat "ask, ask, ask".

Improve Your Skills in 28 Days or Less

To improve your listening, you'll need to make your own action plan that includes:

- Looking for where you need to do better. The quiz you did earlier highlighted opportunities to improve. Or maybe something else has jumped out at you as you've read this book. It's important you commit to action if you want to listen well, so write for yourself the aspect of listening you want to work on.
- Set your intention, in all your conversations, to build the habit Stephen Covey recommends: "Seek first to understand". Use the hand tool to help you.
- Train your brain to be present rather than wander off. Use its excess capacity for noticing nonverbal communication. You don't need to worry about what to say, because you simply focus on them and reflect what you hear.
- With any skill, or change of habit, it's going to feel awkward and hard at first. You'll slip back into old patterns. The antidote is practice, practice, practice until the new way become the default, second nature, easy.
- Acknowledge listening and notice it. Notice it in yourself and give yourself a mental "pat on the back" when you listen well. Notice it in others and show appreciation. Behaviour that is rewarded tends to be repeated. The most simple and effective reward is acknowledgement.

7
GOOD QUESTIONS

Great mentors ask more questions than they answer. They are slow to give advice. Mentors do not withhold their wisdom, but they will draw out their mentee's own thoughts first.

The mantra for mentors could be:

Ask before you tell. Listen, before you speak.

Why Questions are Critical

As mentors, we can empower people by helping them see options, make choices, and take responsibility for their decisions. We move mentoring to a higher level when we recognise adults are masters of their own destiny and they predict the future by what they do now.

Answering your questions enables the mentee to think, create, decide, grow and change in positive ways of their own choosing. In this way, mentors see the reality of Plutarch's statement: "The mind is not a vessel to be filled but a fire to be kindled"

Questions are the foundation of the mentoring conversation. We want people to reflect on experience, make informed decisions, plan and implement action.

At the heart of the mentoring conversation are the four questions outlined in chapter 1. These are not the questions you ask, but the questions you hold in your mind to frame appropriate questions for your particular conversation.

1. **Where are you now?** You want mentees to reflect and talk about themselves and their experience. You literally want to find out where they're coming from in terms of their values, priorities, needs and wants. Your questions help them think.
2. **Where do you want to be?** You invite them to create possibilities and alternatives, comparing and contrasting the current situation and their ideal one. You may provide information and draw on their knowledge. Your questions help them decide and set their goals.
3. **How might you get there?** This will involve growth and change. Your questions get them to come up with strategies and plan actions to progress.
4. **How are you doing?** Is a review question as they implement actions and learn. Your questions let them take stock and adjust.

I want to focus on the first question, where are you now, because, as mentors, we're likely pretty good at leading conversations about goal setting and action planning. I want to encourage you to use more questions early to build the mentee's self-awareness.

There is evidence that suggests greater self-awareness leads to more confidence and creativity, sounder decisions, stronger relationships, more effective communication, more promotions and satisfaction at work, and more effective leadership. Your questions build the mentee's self-awareness.

To develop our understanding of where they are now and to increase their self-awareness, we want to use questions to explore their strengths, past successes, joy, energy, and values.

Here are some examples:

"Describe your 3 greatest talents."

"What brings you joy/most satisfaction/energises you?"

"Who are your role models? What attributes do you admire in them and appreciate most?"

More You Can Do With Questions

The questions listed above are what's known as Appreciative Inquiry. Based on Positive Psychology, they are questions that assist people to appreciate positive aspects of themselves, their experience and their abilities, and use that appreciation to explore their aspirations and opportunities for the future.

This takes mentoring to a higher level. We move from problem-solving to positive change; from a deficit model (something's wrong) to a collaborative approach that identifies and amplifies potential. It offers an empowering context to mentoring, where we guide mentees' progress by expanding options and providing opportunities for self-discovery and positive action.

Sara Olem, Jacqueline Binkert, Ann Clancy, provide a comprehensive guide and examples in their book *Appreciative Coaching*. Their process is highly compatible with the Mentoring Conversation model we looked at earlier.

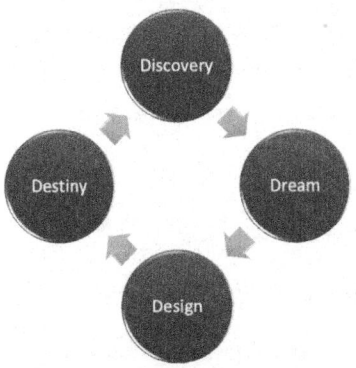

Figure 30: *Appreciative Coaching (Source: Sara Olem, Jacqueline Binkert, Ann Clancy (2007). Jossey-Bass)*

Mentees generally have some sort of topic or area as a focus for the mentoring. If you're part of a mentoring program, it will have some aims that guide you.

Discovery

The purpose is for both mentor and mentee to gain clarity on the mentee's strengths and attributes to build on. So questions will be about their talents and how they've used them in past success. The mentor listens for words, metaphors, hints as to the mentee's values, and clues to their priorities and preferences.

Sample Questions:

"Describe your three greatest accomplishments to date."

"What made these accomplishments stand out for you?"

"What strengths helped you then that you use now?"

List some sample questions of your own:

Dream

The dream phase invites the mentee to speak from the heart about their personal aspirations.

Here we're looking for the context for setting goals. We seek the bigger picture of what they want, their desired future. So you can see why we need to uncover values and priorities early. We'll keep checking in with them as we ask questions about their desired future.

Sample Questions

"Ideally, where do you see yourself in the future?"

"What other possibilities would please you?"

"How does that align with your values of...?"

Design

Now we firm up goals. We want them to get more specific in describing outcomes and we want to build their confidence by affirming their potential. So we ask questions about what success looks like and identify 2-3 major priorities they'll commit to working on. Again, you'll circle back to the discovery phase to link the talents they used in past success to present and future actions. Ask them how they can apply strengths they used then, to their dream.

Sample Questions:

"How will you know you've succeeded? What will you see/feel/experience?"

"What are the most important areas to work on?"

"How could you use your talent of... in this context?"

Destiny

I confess I'm a little uncomfortable with the name of this phase. In earlier versions of Appreciative Inquiry, it was called delivery and personally I'd be happier with that because this phase is about experimentation: you find out what works and do more of that; find out what doesn't work and stop doing that. It means adjustment, creating and living a new reality.

The mentor's purpose in the Destiny/Delivery phase is to expand the mentee's capacity to realise and live a new reality.

Ask questions to encourage experimentation, recognise changes, provide positive reinforcement, and support the mentee through disruption (any change, even positive change, upsets the status quo, and the system has to adjust to a new "normal").

You also want the mentee to build skills for self-reliance. Mentoring should not foster dependence but create independence.

Sample Questions:

"What is changing for you? In what new ways are you thinking and acting"

"What positive results are these changes bringing?"

"How might you apply your skills to manage (a challenge/setback)?"

The Art of Asking

Sigmund Freud said: "The mind is like an iceberg. It floats with one seventh its bulk above the water." In mentoring, our questions raise the mentee's self-awareness, bringing thoughts, feelings, ideas, aspirations from the deep to the surface. We want them to recognise what they want and check its alignment with their values by getting them to talk about why they want it. However, I want you to have alternative ways to ask "why", because asking people why they want something, why they do something or think something is problematic.

Asking a person "why" often:

- Triggers defensiveness and justification
- Focuses on fears, shortcomings and insecurities
- Entrenches mindset, keeping them stuck

Alternatives to "Why"

Instead of:

Why do you want that?

"What is it about that is important for you?"

Instead of:

Why do you feel that way?

"What situations cause you to feel that way?"

Instead of:

Why did you get that bad rating?

"What might you do to get a better rating?"

You need to ask a lot of questions without it ever seeming like an interrogation. And you need to listen well and without judgment, so that they feel safe to keep talking. So I want to finish with some techniques that make that easier.

Cushions - Softening a Confronting Question

Combine these phrases with rapport-building, non-verbal communication to preface a confronting question and soften it. Your approach should be respectful curiosity. This reduces the chance of sounding like an interrogator.

"I'm curious..."

"I'm wondering ..."

"Would you like to tell me...?"

Probing - Getting A Person To Talk More

"Can you say a little more about..."

"Would you expand on that idea..."

"Perhaps you'd like to tell me…"

Summarising—Checking for Understanding

"So, what you're saying is…"

"What I'm hearing is…"

"From your point of view …"

More Sample Questions

To start exploration, ask:

"What factors are affecting on the situation?"

"How do they affect the situation?"

"What are the implications?"

"Why change?"

To facilitate learning, ask:

"What do we know?"

"Are these facts or assumptions?"

"What else do we need to know?"

"What could be different?"

"What are realistic goals?"

To guide planning, ask:

"What are the desired outcomes?"

"How might you achieve these goals?"

"What actions would you need to take?"

"What might be the consequences of the actions contemplated?"

"How will it be done?"

"What resources will you need?"

"How will you monitor progress?"

"When will you begin?"

To support experimentation, ask:

"How is it going?"

"Are adjustments needed?"

"Are the expected outcomes being produced?"

"Are there unexpected outcomes?"

"What would you do differently next time?"

Open Questions

Most of us are familiar with the "open" questions (those that begin with who, what, where, how or when) that help elicit information and "closed" questions, that usually get a "yes" or "no" response.

Diagnostic Questions

Diagnostic questions are aimed at finding the root of a problem, separating symptoms from causes, probing issues and prompting reflection on experience. Examples include:

"Why do you think they responded that way?"

"What happened immediately before this event?"

"What other factors are contributing to the situation?"

"How do you feel about that?"

Information Seeking Questions

There is often a need to gather facts and perceptions in a mentoring conversation. It is also important not to make assumptions and not to move into problem solving until you're sure you have a real understanding of the situation. Questions might include:

"How did you respond to that?"

"What did you do about this?"

"What options have you considered?"

Challenging Questions

One advantage of having a dialogue with a mentoring partner is to explore alternate points of view. Examples of challenging questions are:

"What are your reasons for saying that?"

"What has led you to that conclusion?"

"Do you think other people would see it that way?"

Action Questions

Mentoring is not just about talking; it is about making informed decisions and acting on them. Prompt action planning by asking:

"What could you do to improve the situation?"

"How might you go about achieving that?"

"What specifically do you plan to do?"

Priority & Sequence Questions

Goals and plans are often not achieved because people feel overwhelmed or don't know where to start. Sorting out what is to be done and in what order can clarify thinking and break the task into manageable chunks.

"What will you do first?"

"What is the next step?"

"Is there a logical order in which to proceed?"

"And after that?"

Prediction Questions

Remaining non-directive can be a challenge. Yet sometimes you may see potential pitfalls in someone else's plan. In big decisions, consideration of possible unforeseen consequences is essential. Therefore, prediction questions are good risk management.

"What are your intended outcomes if you take this course of action?"

"What are the likely consequences of this?"

"Potentially, are there other repercussions?"

"If you do nothing, what will happen?"

How to Improve Your Skills

- Set your intention. In all your conversations, aim to build the habit Stephen Covey recommends: "Seek first to understand".
- Build your repertoire of questions. Rephrase or reinvent the samples in this book using your own words.
- Build a new habit. Catch yourself about to give advice and ask questions instead.
- Notice and acknowledge good questions. Notice the results when you use more questions and give yourself a mental "pat on the back".

8

RISK MANAGEMENT

As a mentor, you need to be aware of and deal with any risks posed by the mentoring relationship. In addition, you want to help your mentee recognise, evaluate, and avoid or manage any risks associated with their planned actions.

I have been involved is some mentoring programs for school students paired with adults, but my major experience is with adults and workplace mentoring. If you are mentoring a child or young person, seek expert guidance. Laws, protocols and requirement for interacting with youth are different in different countries and states. You need to be fully aware of these, especially if you are not in a mentoring program that provides structure and guidance.

If you are in a structured program, you can expect to be provided with a mentoring agreement, code of conduct and other guidelines. Most programs supply support from administrators, systems, and procedures that protect mentors and mentees. There is monitoring and troubleshooting, and often, networking with other mentors for mutual help and encouragement. A mentoring program should have the training and backup you need.

The diagram below shows a simple risk management process that I shared with participants in my workshops. I'd have the whole group brainstorm things that could go wrong. Then divide the list and have them work in smaller groups to list how they might prevent these events. Recognising that you can't prevent every risk, they would then describe how they could reduce the impact, should the event occur. Finally, they formulated a back-up plan or action of last resort. This was an effective group process, but you can use it to frame your thinking and conversations with your mentee about managing and dealing with risks.

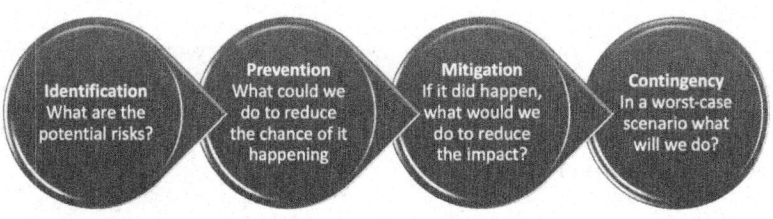

Figure 31: A Simple Risk Management Process for Mentoring

Risks for Mentors

- Physical risk—danger of actual harm
- Emotional risk—fostering a relationship that is too close or inappropriate
- Issues beyond the scope of mentoring
- Acting as a sponsor rather than a mentor
- Dependence—the mentee is not empowered, relies on the mentor, and does not take responsibility

- Conflict—clashing values, opinions or a power struggle
- Unmet expectations—unclear or conflicting assumptions about mentoring

Physical Risk

There is a slight chance of physical risk. I've never known this to happen in any mentoring relationship or program that I've been involved in here in Australia. However, some mentoring programs aim to support people in very challenging personal circumstances, so we should not be complacent.

Never put yourself or your mentee in danger of actual harm. Choose safe, public, places to meet that still give you privacy for your conversation. Online/video meetings are effective and convenient if both parties have the technology.

Emotional Risk

Mentoring is a close relationship in which you're going to discuss personal, not just professional, issues. Together, you may explore the mentee's hopes and dreams, values, needs, wants, challenges, problems, their past and future. You want them to trust you and you want to be worthy of their trust. You must take care that you both respect relationship boundaries. A mentoring program will address this, but in an informal mentoring relationship, set boundaries, assess and perhaps reassess and allow them to evolve or not.

Some mentorship develops into friendship, and such a relationship between equals is not a problem. However, there can be danger where there is a power imbalance—such as a someone in a more senior role with a more junior person, an older mentor with younger mentee, or when the mentor is a position to influence the future of the mentee. You also need to be careful of potential romantic or sexual developments. These are entirely inappropriate and you need to guard against finding yourself in a potentially compromising situation.

If you are mentoring informally, look to professional codes of conduct, organisational policies, and business etiquette. Hold yourself to the highest standards of behaviour and resist becoming too familiar or intimate with your mentee.

A mentor is a confidante. You want to develop trust and openness that allows the mentee to confide in you. They should be able to speak in confidence, knowing that you will not disclose the content of your conversations. Some programs will have a contract with a confidentiality clause and leaders will discuss it in the training or guidelines you receive. However, if you have an informal mentoring relationship, you'll need to talk about confidentiality, and it should work both ways. You may decide to share some personal experience that is useful to your mentee, but that you do not want to go further, so it is important to agree to confidentiality from the start. You cannot completely guard against the mentee breeching confidentiality, but it will help if you preface any sensitive self-disclosure with a gentle reminder:

"between you and me"

"I wouldn't want this to go further."

"I tell you this in confidence."

You may also reassure them of your commitment to confidentiality from time to time as well.

It is important to make explicit the limits of confidentiality. A mentor is not a doctor, lawyer or priest. If a mentee shares information that you are legally bound, or compelled because of your organisation's or the program's policies, to reveal the mentee needs to know this from the beginning. This would include information about intended self-harm or harm to others, unlawful activities, information about harassment, bullying, or sexual misconduct.

Issues Beyond the Scope of Mentoring

Try to establish the scope of your mentoring relationship from the start. Talk about what the mentee wants to discuss and do during your time together. You are free to reconsider and renegotiate the scope, but it is wise to have some agreements as you begin.

You and your mentee need to recognise the limits of your expertise. Unless you are a lawyer, you can have no input on legal matters. If you're not a psychologist, you are not qualified to counsel a mentee on psychological issues. You are a mentor, not a therapist. Do not attempt to deal with drug, alcohol, marital or love relationships, child rearing, health or similar issues. Always refer the mentee to qualified professionals for specialist matters.

If the mentee is dealing with difficulties with coworkers or their manager, tread cautiously. Recognise that you are hearing a subjective version of events. Treat it with respect and acceptance, but with a realistic understanding that it is just one perspective. Accept their view, but do not offer criticism of, or defend, other people involved. Instead, help them process their feelings and assist them to determine if they need to take action. Help them consider options and make plans.

Sponsorship/Mentorship

Many of the mentoring programs I've been involved with have been in Australian government organisation, where equity, fairness and a level playing field for opportunity are core policies. This means organisational programs must guard against giving some people unfair advantage over others. I have some discomfort as I write that last sentence because I know that in most organisations today, there are people who do have an unfair advantage and others who are disadvantaged. If that were not so, we would not need equity and diversity programs!

We often design mentoring to counter the disadvantage experienced by women, disabled people or minority groups. My view is that disadvantaged people actually need sponsorship more than mentoring because their challenges are structural (built in to the system) and unconscious bias (attitudes of the people with power). Mentoring, in this case, may suggest the problem is some deficiency in the disadvantaged group rather than the organisation and the culture. Mentoring in these circumstances can provide a supportive environment for participants, but won't fix the problem.

As a mentor you need to know the difference between mentoring and sponsorship and decide which is appropriate for your situation, or whether you can accommodate both.

Mentors	Sponsors
Have mentees	Have protégés
Listens, asks, elicits the mentee's needs and wants, values and vision	Helps drive protégé's vision and goals
Provides support and encouragement	Invested in protégé's advancement
Share strategies the mentee can use to connect to high profile projects and people	Uses influence to connect protégé to opportunities, high profile projects and people
Suggests ways the mentee can expand and use their own network	Provides access to their network, opens doors, make introductions
Discusses ways the mentee can gain visibility and beneficial experiences	Champions their protégé, helping them gain visibility and exposure to beneficial experiences
Encourage mentee to apply for positions, promotions and pay rises they are qualified for and help them prepare to pitch their case	Will help protégé access positions, promotions and pay rises
Coaches the mentee to advocate for themself	Advocates for the protégé

Figure 32: Mentors/Sponsors

Dependence

The whole purpose of mentoring is to empower the mentee—enable them to have the confidence and capability to act on their own behalf, to make decisions that are right for them, become stronger, access and use resources, exercise their own influence, become autonomous, take control and responsibility for their life and direction. To achieve that, you need to make them do the thinking, ensure they equip themselves to achieve their goals and work out their own solutions.

Acting for them, answering their every question and too quickly giving them advice robs them of power and can make them dependent on you, and resentful if things go wrong. They may run to you with problems they could solve themselves, fail to take responsibility for their actions, and blame you for failure or adverse results. Don't do it!

Conflict

There is great value in divergent views, but in mentoring we want a productive exchange of ideas, not conflict. Scientific research shows that difference, dissent and discordant ideas actually make us smarter. If we can overcome our own discomfort and defensiveness and really hear a different perspective, we can bring more intelligence to decision-making. So mentors need to set the tone of conversations to enable multiple points of view.

Mentors and mentees do not have to agree. They may have different values or beliefs, and it is easier to accept these ideas if we recognise them as opinions, not truth or fact. A mentoring relationship is not a contest of ideas, we don't have to defend our views or refute someone else's. We simply facilitate the mentee's exploration of *their* beliefs so that *they* can decide if beliefs serve them and want to use them to guide their actions.

Personality clashes and incompatibility are often cited as reasons to dissolve a mentoring relationship, and if a pair really can't work productively together, then it is better to disengage. Mentoring programs should have a no fault, opt out process. Sometimes a mentee or mentor who doesn't get along with one person does fantastically well with another, but we have to face the fact that not everyone is cut out to be a mentor or mentee. If it's not working out, don't ghost your partner, that is fail to return calls, emails or message or attend scheduled meetings. Be upfront about your unwillingness to continue. If you are in a mentoring program, seek help from coordinators to reallocate the mentee and provide them with support, which may include some corrective feedback.

Unmet Expectations

Unmet expectations are by far the most frequent cause of dissatisfaction in mentoring and the easiest to prevent or resolve.

There are lots of different definitions of mentoring and people have a variety of views about what it is and the way it should work. If you are in a structured program, there will be a clear description of mentoring aims, roles, responsibilities, protocols, and guidelines. Often, there is a mentoring agreement to be signed by the mentor and mentee. You can use these documents in an early conversation and explore the mentee's expectations and yours. If you are mentoring informally, it is best to discuss expectations at the beginning and review regularly.

Mentoring relationships unfold, they grow and change. There is usually enough flexibility to review and renegotiate your mentoring relationship. If the mentee has expectations beyond your means or willingness to meet, and a candid discussion cannot resolve the differences, it may be necessary to part ways. Try to do this respectfully and amicably.

Helping Mentees Manage Risks

You are leading mentoring conversations aimed at enabling the mentee to make decisions and act on them. Sometimes you may see a significant downside to their decision, a potential risk that they may not see. It would be irresponsible not to help them realise unforeseen consequences.

Alerting them to possible negative outcomes will work better if you can ask questions that allow them to gain this insight themselves. This will be easier if you have fostered their ability to look at different points of view.

"When you do X, what are the outcomes you expect?"

"Are there other possible results?"

"How do you think others may react?"

"What negative consequences do you imagine may be possible?"

"What else could happen?"

The mentee may have less experience than you, and they still may not imagine the consequence you foresee. Then, you have a duty of care to let them know. It will still be their choice to proceed or not, but you want them to make an informed decision, so give them the information they need.

"I have some concerns about that course of action. May I share them?"

"In my experience, I have found that when you do X, Y seems to follow, and after that comes Z."

"So, I'm thinking that if you do that, it might cause…"

Overall, a philosophy of risk management that has served me well in life is:

- Expect the best, but plan for the worst.
- Focus on the outcomes you want.
- What you do and what you don't do has consequences.
- Take responsibility for your own actions.

PART III
SKILLS FOR LEADER-MENTORS

9

LEADING LEARNING

Mentoring is a way of leading learning. We want our mentee to develop and grow. So, I want to start with a concept I call "learning Ladders".

From an early age, we love to climb. We love playgrounds that allow us to learn and strengthen our skills. Our desire for mastery continues in adulthood. Mastery is one of our strongest intrinsic drives. Particular interests attract us, called by innate talents and potential that ignite a desire to learn. Learning ladders take us from where we are to where we want to be, they provide the steps to mastery. Something to reach for. Something to hang on to. Something to step up to. Something for support.

Figure 33: Learning Ladder

The first rung of a learning ladder is having **something to reach for**, a reason, a need to move or grow. People do not reach out without motivation or inspiration. It might be an external drive to action, to move away from pain or strive for reward. Pain might include peer pressure, shame, or compulsion to bravado. However, inspiration touches the soul, connects with the heart and mind, it is influenced from the core of one's being. It may come with an "ah ha" of sudden insight, or slower dawning self-knowledge from within that sets us on a mission.

Climbing is a risk. It means change, moving from the known into the unknown. This triggers some level of uncertainty—a healthy and positive anticipation, a reasonable expectation of success; or anxiety, unhelpful doubts, fears, memories, or imaginings of failure. So, the second rung of a learning ladder is **something to hang on to**. Security in the form of a solid framework, building on what you already know, recognise, or have established. This makes it safer to reach across the gap from the known to the unknown.

The third rung of the learning ladder is **something to step up to**. An aspiration, something new, attractive, better than the present state of being. A belief that there is a genuine opportunity to progress and reach a higher station. Knowledge that it is possible, role models or examples that show how similar others have achieved desired results. Confidence that goals are achievable.

The fourth rung of the learning ladder is **something for support**. Resources or a program to keep development on track. Feedback that provides positive reinforcement of progress, as well as constructive redirection when needed. Most of all, support can be provided by other people. A team behind you, a cohort of peers alongside you, leaders, champions, mentors, and coaches on your side.

If you want to lead learning, you need to put ladders in place.

Learning at Work

Learning in the workplace is more that training courses. It may be may be surprising to know that just 10% of workplace learning comes from formal education and training. 20% comes from exposure. This is social learning from and with colleagues, peers, team collaboration, personal learning networks, leaders, mentors, and coaches. Then, as much as 70%, comes from experience—doing day-to-day tasks, taking on a new challenge or project, practicing techniques.

Education includes formal education and training that usually takes place off-the-job, such as conferences, courses, workshops, seminars, usually face-to-face but increasingly online. And if you're like me, maybe you're wondering why this type of learning is only the 10%. After all, we've seen an increase in e-learning. Some of it is great, with engaging simulations and gamification, but some are not much more than a boring electronic book with multiple-choice questions to check they've read it.

Exposure (social learning) family, peers, teachers, community, society, role-models, coaches, mentors and leaders can be a positive or a negative. Social learning is powerful. You can reflect on the ways the influence of these have been a positive or a negative for you.

Experience could be called "learning by doing". People learn how to do routine tasks and, as they practice, they become more competent. Their experience may make them more confident, capable, and quicker. More than that, they may figure out more efficient ways to get the job done. Systems of continuous improvement are built on the understanding that workers' experience allows them to see possibilities for efficiencies and greater effectiveness. Japan is a leader in this field. One reason the quality of cars has gone up while costs have come down is worker input to improve production lines.

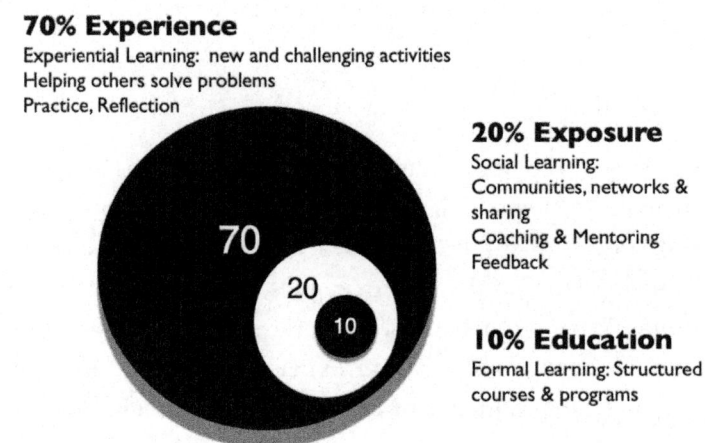

70% Experience
Experiential Learning: new and challenging activities
Helping others solve problems
Practice, Reflection

20% Exposure
Social Learning:
Communities, networks & sharing
Coaching & Mentoring
Feedback

10% Education
Formal Learning: Structured courses & programs

Figure 34: 70:20:10

70 20 10 isn't an either/or choice. Workplace learning can be integrated. For example, one graduate program I was involved in was a combination of all three. Graduates did a diploma externally, in-house courses, and career development workshops plus mentoring and job rotations. Managers were tasked to develop required competencies by setting work assignments for on-the-job learning aligned with the diploma course, and their mentor asked to support career and personal development. The graduates took responsibility for the overall process with a graduate program manager checking in.

So, let's have a look at how we can improve and integrate 70 20 10 and where mentoring fits. Mostly, mentoring is thought of in the 20% slice of the pie. I take a holistic view - you can't get full value from the 70, 20 or the 10 without mentoring and coaching.

Education 10: Although it represents the smallest part of the 70 20 10 equation, formal education and training is the most expensive part of workplace learning. It used to include the cost of taking people away from the workplace, travel and accommodation and course or conference fees. As we return to large-scale events, employers will be far more exacting about getting a good return on investment. Increasingly, we've embraced technology for online presentations. They are convenient, less expensive and can be effective, but that's not guaranteed.

Challenges to Education

- Too many are boring lectures and death by PowerPoint!
- Overloaded with information
- Poor transfer of learning
- Questionable cost-effectiveness
- Fatigue from frequent online meetings
- Distractions and stress

Learning is not effective if it is not used! The sad fact is that transfer of learning is very low. Problems start with short-term and long-term memory. **Most of us have very poor retention.** As shown in the Forgetting Curve (next page). In the good old days of in-person training, we could design lots of practice in our training and take the time to embed learning with repetition and recall exercises.

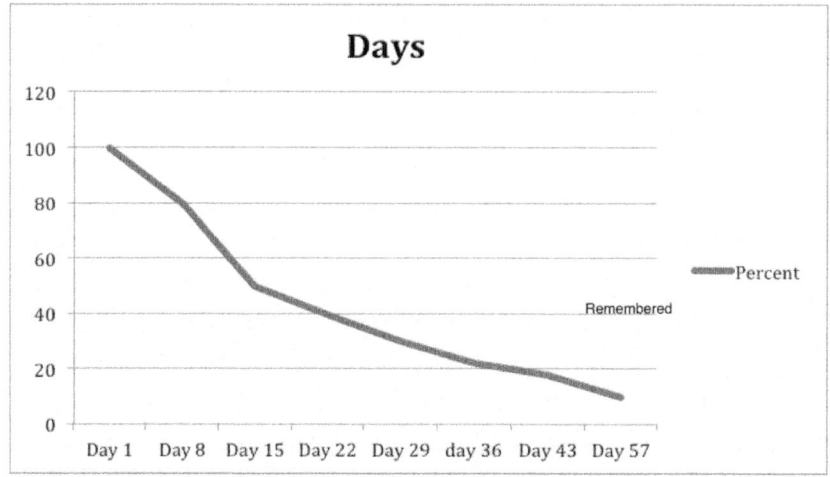

Figure 35: Forgetting Curve. Source: *MLA (7th ed.)* ***Ebbinghaus, Hermann.*** *Memory; a Contribution to Experimental Psychology. New York city: Teachers college, Columbia University, 1913.*

However, it's not *just* the quantity or quality of off-site or online delivery that determines the value of education; it's what happens before and after in the work environment.

As a mentor or manager, you can help boost the effectiveness of education and training because we apply very little learning in the workplace in any meaningful way, without coaching or mentoring. You can discuss the purpose of off-the-job education before the learner goes. You can talk about why they're going, what the objectives and expected benefits are, how it is relevant to their work now and in the future. Flag that you will have follow-up conversations. These will include talking about outcomes, actions, support, and plans for ongoing feedback.

Best Practice for the "10" Education (Off-the-job learning)

- Provide engaging pre and post learning activities
- Plan with employees before and after any off-the-job learning event

- Compliment all training and education with mentoring and coaching
- Empower employees to manage their own development and support proactive learners.

Let's have a deeper look at exposure—social learning. People learn from the norms presented to them by colleagues in the workplace, so exposure to the right role models is vital. We absorb attitudes, values and behaviours from our environment. Employees need leaders they can emulate, who show interest and take time to develop them. Investing in on-boarding for new hires is so important and mentors can convey the vision, mission and culture.

Proactive learners seek feedback, people with whom to debrief, or bounce ideas off. They will reach outside the workplace, using online networks and people in close proximity. These employees are likely to be your organisation's best talent. As a mentor or manager, if you can engage them, you're more likely to keep them.

We are talking about people who are likely to be confident, hungry for development opportunities and mobile. Conversations with a mentor or a leader with mentoring skills are critical if you are to retain them. Ensure that you acknowledge their self-directed learning and help them put it to good use.

Best Practice for the "20" Exposure

- Commit to your role as a mentor for learning
- Mentor new hires, graduate recruits and interns
- Develop your mentoring and coaching skills
- Model "Everyone, Always, Learning"

Show proactive learners how to get the most from personal learning networks and mentors

Most workplace learning (70%) comes from experience—doing day-to-day tasks, taking on a new challenge or project. However, we **only**

learn from experience when activate the learning cycle. We have an experience. We pause to reflect, decide to do something different, and act on that decision.

I often ask my face-to-face groups: Have you ever made a mistake? Of course, most hands go up, but a guy once said: "I thought I did once, but I was wrong!" Someone else said: there's no such thing as a mistake, only a learning experience. But you know people who *don't* learn from their mistakes—don't even realise they've made one. You can't learn from experience unless you pause and reflect and even that won't make a difference unless you make an informed decision —choose to take action.

There's evidence that we learn even more when we reflect on our successes. Yet we stop to reflect infrequently. Leadership is critical to experiential learning. Leaders must build relationships and *invite* the learner to reflect on their experience. If there's no reflection, there's no lesson. You want people to gain insight from their experience that can improve performance. So, whether it's positive reinforcement of what they did well, corrective guidance, or simply noticing whether they are learning the right things—or learning at all—a conversation with a mentor adds value.

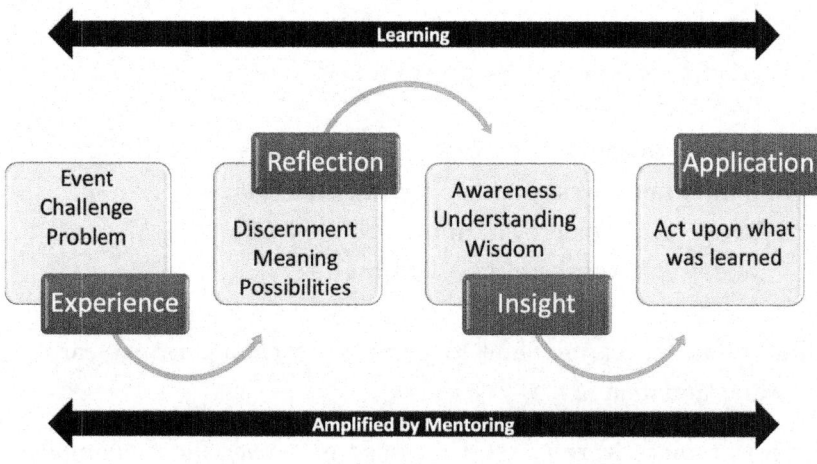

Figure 36: Mentoring Amplifies Learning

Mentoring amplifies learning from on-the-job experience, a challenge, problem, or success when you lead a conversation that causes a person to reflect on experience. What does it mean? What possibilities does it open? Thinking and reflection can cause insight, awareness, understanding, an ah ha moment, or epiphany. And, as a mentor, you encourage them to act on what they learn.

Best Practice for the "70" Experience:

- Start conversations to review events, challenges, problems and successes. Make it a habit, do it regularly. Take the time. It will pay off and save you time in the long run.
- Be curious, collaborative, concerned. Ask questions that cause people to reflect. You need to have them know you are not looking to blame and shame them for things that have gone wrong; you're interested in preventing problems in the future.
- Facilitate insight—you want the ideas to come from them if possible. Be patient and look for the "ah ha" moment. You'll see it on their face.
- Gain their commitment to act on what they've learned from the experience. Ask them what they need from you to do so. They may need more guidance, modelling or coaching. People need support to perform and the skills and knowledge to do the job.
- Feedback is critical, looking back at what was done, how it was done, and how it might be improved. Follow-up and offer praise—if they've done well, acknowledge their effort or help them correct their course if they've gone off-track.

So, mentors and leaders who have mentoring and coaching conversations add value to all three areas of learning, the 70, the 20 and the 10. Leading learning in the workplace means you:

- Activate learning from experience by causing people to reflect on past experience and decide what to do in the future.
- Help them get the right learning from exposure.
- Lead by example; you are a role model; you share tips and tricks, give practical guidance and you encourage their use of other mentors, peer and personal learning networks.
- Leverage education (off-the-job learning) by discussing what you expect them to gain and why that's important before the training; and how it will be used and supported back on the job after the event.

10

FEEDBACK

I wrote this chapter with team leaders and managers in mind, but it applies to one-on-one mentoring as well as other group situations.

Feedback is one of the most powerful communication tools you have.

Effective feedback affirms and reinforces behaviour; or encourages someone to think or do something differently. I would go so far to say that in most cases, you have a duty to provide feedback.

Positive feedback can provide encouragement. It can build a person's sense of self-worth, and it can foster a good relationship between you and them. And, corrective feedback—when you let someone know that what they are doing is not what you want—can also encourage, build their self-worth and foster your relationship, if you do it well.

If you feel uncomfortable giving feedback, you are not alone. Mark Murphy, of Leadership IQ, sampled 30,000 employees and found: "Around nine out of ten managers have avoided giving constructive feedback to their employees for fear of the employees reacting poorly." That may be why, according to Gallup, 28% of employees say they receive feedback only a few times a year, while 19% say they receive feedback once a year or less.

In terms of the effectiveness of the feedback, this might come as a shock to you. In a meta-analysis of the effects of feedback on performance, Kluger and DeNisi[1] found that feedback does nothing or makes things worse more often than it improves performance.

Only 14% of employees say that performance reviews inspire them to improve[2]. Funnily enough, only 14% of organisations are actually happy with their performance management systems[3]! Bryant Ott[4] put it this way, "Traditional performance management puts off until tomorrow what can benefit employees and the team today."It is clear, we must give feedback and we must get better at it.

To make feedback easier, more enjoyable and even more effective, what we need to do is:

- Help others become less fearful of feedback
- Get the ratio of positive and corrective feedback right
- Give feedback with the right frequency
- Build a culture of trust
- Model seeking and accepting feedback

Of course, not everyone fears feedback. Sports people rely on measures of performance and strive for their PB (personal best) using it as motivation to win and sometimes to cope with a loss. However, neuroscientists tell us that feedback about performance can feel threatening.

> "Feedback about performance, in particular, activates the brain's primary threat network, which produces a feeling akin to physical pain."
>
> David Rock & Beth Jones (2017) Want to Kill Your Performance Ratings? Here's How to Ensure Success. Strategy and Business blog

Fear may be a result of previous experience and traditional ratings-based appraisal, where ranking and labelling triggers the fight/flight/freeze reaction in the brain. An emotional response is difficult to overcome and to deal with.

Some managers and organisations have transformed the feedback process, making it positive and productive, reducing fear and discomfort.

Here are 4 tips for making feedback less fearful:

1. Make sure feedback has a future focus
2. Use reflection as a tool for learning (see previous chapter)
3. Establish individual goals
4. Prepare and practice

A Future Focus

You can't change the past, but you can alter present behaviour to improve performance. So, when assessment, rankings, rating and labels are *not* part of the conversation and you focus on the future, feedback can be less threatening.

Use feedback to establish expectations. It seems astonishing but the studies have found that only 50% of employees clearly know what's expected of them at work!

If you lead a team, you absolutely must have clear and continuing conversations with teams and individuals about expectations, including:

- The team mission
- Organisation values
- Outcomes and measures
- Performance standards

In a high functioning team under a good leader, you address these in regular team meetings. Team members take an active role, presenting information, discussing and suggesting actions for improvement, and accepting accountability for implementing them.

One construction manager I knew was renowned for bringing projects in on time and under budget. His primary tool was the project debrief team meeting. Conducted as a non-threatening review, he led a conversation about what worked and what did not, without praise or blame.

You can take the shame out of failure, mistakes, or poor performance without reducing accountability by using this kind of feedback. Then deciding, collaboratively, what needs to be done differently and getting commitment to change.

I've included a *Team Productivity Checklist* in the Guides at the back of this book. It details these areas and more. Its from my ebook: *How to Lift Team Productivity* .You can download a free copy here: https://dl.bookfunnel.com/ji85sra3yc

Individualise Goals

Team feedback can be powerful, inclusive, and motivating. Complement this with individualised goals that are linked to the team's goals and reflect each individual's role. They will have different levels of development and different strengths, so you'll need to have individual conversations with them.

Sometimes our own fear and emotion can get in the way. So, we need to prepare ourselves. Recall giving or receiving feedback that was positive and productive. Put yourself in a state of calm, mentor mode. Practice your communication techniques, listening and asking good questions. Don't expect to be perfect immediately, especially if this approach is new for you and your team. Have patience with yourself and with them as you adapt, but persist. You must be consistent and continue the process. Point out positive change.

Even done well, feedback is not always going to be a positive experience, but we must make it as positive as we can, because as discussed in chapter 3, we need positivity to outweigh negativity in our lives and in our workplaces if we are to flourish. If the ratio is out of whack, relationships suffer, teams don't function well, and people are less productive. Barbara Fredrickson talks about this in her evidence-based book: *Positivity*. She's not just advocating "positive thinking" and affirmations here, but experiencing heartfelt emotions like hope, pride, amusement, inspiration, interest, awe, gratitude, serenity, joy and love as opposed to: fear, anger, sorrow, alarm, panic, indifference, contempt, shame, guilt, remorse. And there is a tipping point where people will languish or flourish. The tipping point is 3:1, more positivity is better, in fact it can get to 15:1 before it becomes too much.

What if I told you there was a simple way to raise positivity in your workplace that has been shown to improve performance on a range of measures?

Ochsner Health Care Services in the US has 11,000 employees and educated all their leaders, physicians, nurses and support staff to implement what they call the 10/5 way[5] and got these bottom-line results: increased unique patient visits, increased their likelihood to recommend the organisation, and significantly improved medical practice provider scores.

10/5 is a way of providing social support to work colleagues and patients—social support has been linked to positive physical and emotional outcomes, employee engagement and productivity. It's really simple. If you walk within 10 feet (roughly 3 metres) of another person, you make eye contact and smile. If you are within 5 feet (around 1.5 metres) feet, you say hello.

If you start doing 10/5 by yourself, or even with your team, it might feel silly and forced in the beginning, but building the habit has personal benefits and business ones. Eye contact, smiling and greeting are the most basic form of feedback, saying: I see you. I respect you. I am not a threat. I care.

Most people in the workplace are not getting enough positive feedback. I was a consultant for over 30 years and people commonly told me they get "sea gull" management—perhaps you've heard of it? It's where managers fly in, poop all over you and fly out again! Hopefully that's not what happens where you work, but I also got comments like "they're quick to tell us when something is wrong… but rarely tell us when we do things right." And that's my point. We need positive feedback *and* corrective feedback, and we need a lot more positive feedback at least three times as much. I once heard the positive feedback likened to the wind in the sails of a yacht, and corrective feedback is like its rudder. Both are vital to sailing the boat on its course.

When providing feedback, there are three types of feedback we can use:

- Affirming: positive feedback on behaviours you want people to keep doing.
- Correcting: behaviours you need them to do differently.
- Reviewing: when you collaborate to find ways to do better.

Typically, people do not get enough affirmation — praise or positive feedback. You may be familiar with Ken Blanchard's adage from *The One Minute Manager*, "catch them doing something right." The trick to improving performance with feedback is getting the right balance of positive and corrective feedback.

I suggest looking for every opportunity to give affirming feedback or praise. In behavioural psychology, this is called positive reinforcement. It ranges from eye contact and a smile, saying "thank you" letting people know you appreciate them, nodding or make a short comment that lets a person know you're listening, giving a compliment, to actual rewards. Compliments must be genuine—people have very good BS detectors, so honesty is vital—and, of course giving praise for good work, effort and achievement. This not only increases the positivity ratio, it also builds trust and rapport and a workplace culture where people feel respected and valued.

As well as reinforcing desirable behaviours, praise increases endorphin levels (the feel-good hormone). It increases oxytocin (a bonding hormone) and reduces stress hormones. Sounds like a good recipe for better relationships to me!

None of this means we ignore below-standard performance at work or inappropriate behaviour. Indeed, we have a duty to stamp out harassment and bullying in our workplaces. An absence of feedback, including consequences, allows people to get away with unacceptable behaviour. As David Morrison, Chief of the Australian Army stated in a powerful speech[6]: "The standard you walk past is the standard you accept". Managers have a responsibility to call out, correct and ensure consequences for behaviours.

A Formula For Effective Feedback

Feedback affirms and reinforces behaviour; or encourages someone to do something different.

1. Start with objective facts: State what the person is doing in specific, behavioural terms.
2. Describe the impact, say why it's important, the difference it makes, or how you feel.
3. Affirm, say thank you, well done to reinforce the positive

The steps are the much the same for corrective feedback, however, I'd add some questions after the impact. There may be a reason or a problem you don't know about and it will be much more productive and better for the relationship to explore that before you take the next step.

Here's an example: a supervisor wanted to change the behaviour of an apprentice, who was consistently late for work. It was not only annoying, but getting to the stage where the apprentice could be sacked if he couldn't become punctual.

Objective Fact: *"You've been late, three times this week."*

Impact: *"If this continues, you're in danger of losing your job."*

It's important that you do not deliver this type of message as a threat. The supervisor wanted to change the behaviour NOT get rid of the employee or punish them. So, the non-verbal message is vital—it's concern, wanting to help solve a problem, positively mentoring the person. Next, the supervisor asks questions that invite problem-solving.

Question: *"I'm wondering what the problem is and why you're having such a hard time getting to work on time?"*

It may seem silly to us, but the young person simply didn't wake up early enough. He set an alarm on his phone, but often, barely awake, would turn it off and fall asleep again. The supervisor asked the apprentice to come up with ways to overcome that, (move the phone out of reach, so he had to get up, set a second or third alarm, go old school with a clock). Together, they agreed a solution, an alternative that would work for both of them. The supervisor closely monitored the situation and reinforced the apprentice's punctuality in the following days with affirming feedback.

Sometimes people are unable or unwilling to negotiate a different approach. In that case, you'll have to instruct them. Explain what you want them to start doing; not just what you need them to stop, because they need to have an alternate behaviour for what they're doing now.

Here are some general guidelines for giving both affirming and corrective feedback:

- Do it as soon as possible. The closer to the event you give feedback, the more it is associated with the behaviour—a cause-and-effect relationship is recognised in the brain.
- Feedback must be sincere. Compliments and concerns must be genuine.

- Be specific. Saying: "Good job" is positive but vague. Adding "what was most effective was x" is better.
- State the benefit, tell the person how what they did affected you or others, for example "Good job. What was most effective was X because Y." Or, "when you are ten minutes late for our meeting, it disrespects the time of every person here." You would make the latter statement to the person privately, not in front of the meeting, and you might first ask questions about valid reasons for their lateness.
- Shape to the person. Some people like rewards, certificates or other symbolic feedback, but others see that as insincere. This is NOT a case of treating people as you would like to be treated, but finding out what they appreciate.
- Share appropriately—you can celebrate wins as a team and etiquette says praise in public; critique in private, but again, not everyone enjoys public praise, so you need to understand their preference.

Collaborative Review

This is where you and others agree there's a need for change and to work together to do so. This works with team or individuals.

- Compare ideal with the real, current situation.
- Identify the gap and why it matters.
- Discuss what needs to change, draw on past experience and strategies that have worked. Brainstorm options.
- Create an action plan.

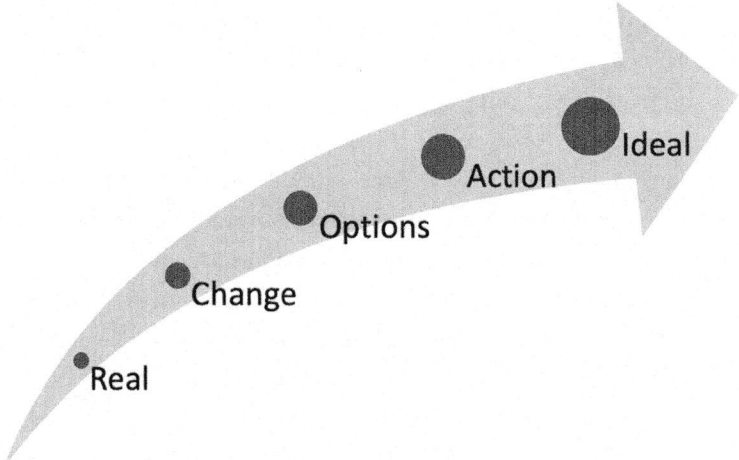

Figure 37: Collaborative Review

Gallup research has found that employees are most engaged when they meet with managers weekly and feedback is on the agenda. You want to help them set priorities and ask them what support they need from you. They've also found being open to discuss non-work topics is important. People need to know you take a personal interest in them, they want to know you care. Younger people want more feedback. Connecting daily with a quick text, email or drop by, checking in but not checking up on them.

Mentoring moments are those times you take the opportunity to have a conversation that creates insight, explores options, or provides guidance while you are doing something else. They happen in the workplace, at home, during leisure activities and extend normal conversation. In mentoring moments, you:

- Notice and acknowledge what they have done.
- Encourage self-reflection.
- It's a check-in, not a check-up. No one like to be micromanaged.
- You might offer support and, if needed, guide and correct.

You want to be a role model of seeking feedback and handling it well when you receive it. You should evaluate feedback that others give you by asking yourself three questions:

1. **What is this person's intention?** Why are they telling me this? If they have good intentions, like your well-being, professional development, better teamwork, patient outcomes, process improvement or other positive intent, it's worth hearing their input.
2. **Is this feedback valid?** It's probably valid from their point of view, but they may not have all the facts, or they may interpret the situation differently from you.
3. **Does this person, situation, or a better outcome, matter to you?** Should you care? I'm sure you know there are people out there that sound off for their own reasons that are nothing to do with you, they have no good intention, say ridiculous things and, as upsetting as they may be, actually they don't matter, unless you allow them to.

If there is good intention, the feedback's valid, and it matters, you then need to ensure the person giving it feels heard, and consider what you might do differently for a better result.

Treat receiving corrective feedback is the same as the collaborative review. Envision what the ideal situation would look like, look at what's happening now (real). Acknowledge the differences between the current reality and an ideal situation. Then, drawing from experience, your strengths, and strategies that might work, look at what is within your power to change. Then create an action plan to take the steps that you are willing and able to do.

How do you respond to affirming feedback, a compliment, praise? Simply: "Thank you" or "I appreciate you saying that".

11

MOTIVATION

We've come a long way since the carrot and stick philosophy of motivation, though there are some still trying to treat us like donkeys!

When we talk about motivating people, we usually mean that we want to get them to think, feel or do something differently.

Dictionary.com talks about motivating as "providing a reason to act in a certain way"; being motivated as "having a strong reason to accomplish something"; and something that motivates as "inducement; incentive".

These definitions assume we make rational decisions to act in certain ways. But that's not so.

Science has established:

- 95-99% of behaviour is unconscious—we're not even aware of any motivation
- We often act against our best interests
- Emotion has at least as much influence as reason on our conscious decisions

99% Unconscious

95-99% of behaviour is merely a habit, actions that we could decide to do differently, but basically do on "auto-pilot". Ever driven a known route and arrived at your destination safely, then realised you have no memory of getting there? Which hand do you hold your fork in? Do you sit in the same chair for every meal at home? There are dozens of things we do each day that are left to habit—learned behaviour, relegated to the subconscious to take care of in order to free our conscious mind for thinking in real time.

Acting against our best interests

If we were totally rational, we'd never over-eat, drink too much, gamble or smoke. We'd exercise and meditate, manage our finances well, and not get ourselves entangled in poor relationships. We wouldn't follow fashion or waste time on cat/dog/goat videos online. There'd be no trolls, no inspiration, and little interest in Kardashians. We'd never get upset by criticism or bask in praise. There would be no heroes risking their lives to rescue others because the head would rule the heart, act in our own self-interest, and do what was best for us.

Emotion has at least as much influence as reason

Emotions trigger neurochemicals in the brain. The strongest emotional reaction is fight/flight/freeze, where any threat activates the amygdala and triggers a primal survival response. Then a flood of neurochemicals causes us to see differently, process differently and behave differently.

The words "motivation" and "emotion" have the same Latin root "mot", to move. So, if you want to motivate yourself or others, you cannot ignore the power of emotions.

Maslow's classic Theory of Human Motivation recognised the power of emotions and can still be useful in understanding motivation in the workplace.

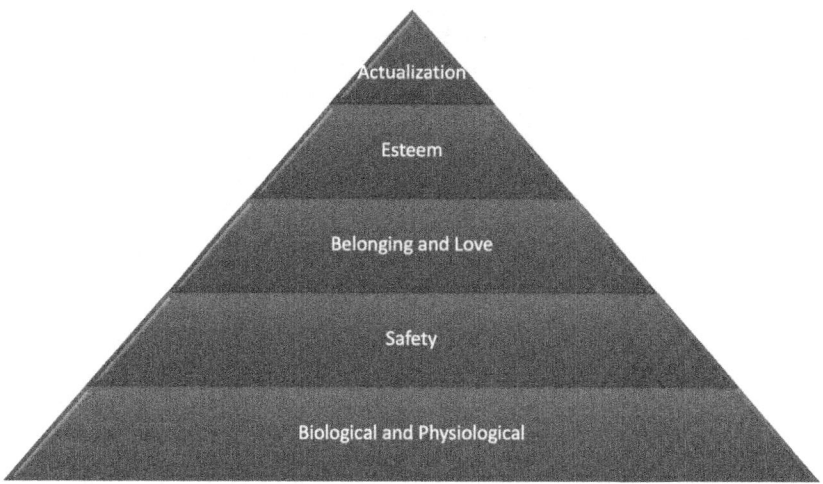

Figure 38: *Abraham Maslow (1943)* A Theory of Human Motivation. *Psychological Review*

If a person's basic needs for food and shelter aren't met (by adequate pay), people do not feel safe (through disrespect, bullying or harassment), they do not feel like they belong (because of racism, sexism, isolation and lack of friendliness), or their esteem is not nurtured (they are treated as low-status, lack recognition and attention) and have no opportunity to accomplish their full potential, you are unlikely to "motivate" them to be more productive. In fact, if the basic safety and belonging needs are not met, *expect* counter-productive behaviour.

If you are a manager, your first task is to ensure the workplace feels safe emotionally as well as physically and employees are valued members of your team.

It's here that managers who mentor differ from off-line mentors—mentors who are not in the line of authority over the mentee and are not responsible for performance and organisational objectives. Managers *do* have a responsibility to create an environment that brings out the employee's best *and* direct their efforts so that they achieve specific outcomes.

Off-line mentors foster the best interests of the mentee; managers who mentor operate in the space where the employee's interest and the organisation's interests overlap.

Managers who mentor are concerned with performance, so the second task is to look at what impedes accomplishment of performance goals. Exploring this is important because there are some things that no amount of "motivation" is going to fix, but there are other ways to get a better result.

It's not always a lack of motivation that prevents performance. Often, there are obstacles of which you are not even aware. So it's important to find out what's actually going on.

Force-field analysis, a team process developed by Kurt Lewin, can be very illuminating. It will engage your team in identifying driving forces—factors that support, encourage or propel people toward the desired situation and restraining forces—all the factors, pressures and issues that restrict progress or prevent the desired situation. Once identified, you can work to reduce restraining forces and boost driving forces. I've included a description of how to conduct force-field analysis in the guides at the back of the book.

You can use force-field analysis in any group (or by yourself) for any goal. Try force-field analysis on one of your own goals. Then use it on a performance goal specific to your team. The process itself is motivating. By engaging your team this way, you have already built real motivation that leads to performance and satisfaction.

Carrot and Stick?

Unfortunately, most workplaces still use the old carrot and stick method of offering rewards, bonuses, commissions for performance and punishment for failure.

In Daniel Pink's book *Drive, The Surprising Truth About What Motivates Us*, he shares "The Seven Deadly Flaws of Carrots and Sticks". Incentives can:

1. **Extinguish intrinsic motivation**—if we are paid to do something we enjoy, it can turn "play" into work. Many replicated experiments have shown that rewarding subjects for tasks they enjoy reduces their inclination to do it! This is a good reason not to pay mentors! Rewards can offend those who volunteer to mentor for altruistic reasons and they may lose enthusiasm.
2. **Diminish performance**—ask any farmer employing fruit pickers where pay is based on amount picked. Quality usually goes down as speed goes up!
3. **Crush creativity**—when compared, artists' commissioned and non-commissioned works showed the same level of technical competence, but the paid artworks to do were less creative.
4. **Crowd out good behaviour**—to reward on-time arrival, parents with children in child-care were fined for late pickup. However, the number arriving late increased! In Hong Kong, car parking is hard to find. Drivers often choose to take a fine for a convenient, but illegal, parking spot.
5. **Encourage cheating**, shortcuts, and unethical behaviour—here in Australia, a Royal Commission has exposed the extent to which paying bonuses and commissions for selling financial services and advice has resulted in appalling behaviour by major banks and investment companies.
6. **Become addictive**—gambling addiction occurs with small and infrequent rewards. Brain studies show that this stimulates the same area of the brain as that associated with the high of drug addiction. On a similar note, pay your child once for doing a chore and they will not only expect payment next time, but they will gradually want more and more pay for their jobs.

7. **Foster short-term thinking**—rewarding your child for studying might get them the grade you want, but will not build any commitment to study.

Sometimes pay for performance may work for example in tasks that require no creativity and very little thinking at all. Incentives can enhance boring, repetitive tasks performed systematically.

In his book, Daniel Pink shares decades of research on motivation. He explains why traditional motivation, including external rewards, seldom works and the three elements that do: build autonomy, mastery and purpose.

- **Autonomy**—the need to direct our own life
- **Mastery**—the intrinsic desire to learn and create new things
- **Purpose**—wanting to do better by ourselves and the world

Autonomy

Some workplaces have had success introducing Results-Only Work Environment (ROWE). Workers have no set work hours, they don't even have to come into work—as long as they get their work done. This may be too radical an idea to apply universally, but there are now millions of people who telecommute. There have always been self-employed people, farmers, artisans and entrepreneurs who have produced with no one managing them!

Studies have shown the powerful impact autonomy has on individual performance. They have shown a greater choice about what you do and how and when you do it to result in:

- Higher productivity
- Conceptual understanding
- Enhanced persistence
- Less burnout
- Psychological wellbeing and

- Job Satisfaction leading to higher performance

What increases autonomy?

- Empathy—seeing issues from their perspective
- Meaningful feedback and information
- Choice about what to do and how to do it
- Encouraging employees to take on new projects

Naturally, for autonomy to work, outcomes must be clear and well defined so that people can be accountable and have that sense of achievement.

Mastery

Intellectual challenge, the urge to master something new and engaging, is the best predictor of productivity. Mastery builds capability and increases employee engagement.

When tasks exceed a person's capabilities, it causes anxiety, but when they are below their capabilities, the result is boredom. Managers need to create **"Goldilocks Tasks"**—challenges that are not too difficult and not too easy, but just right for the person.

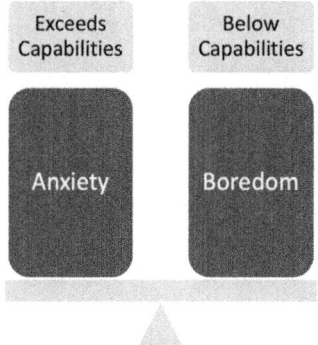

Figure 40: Goldilocks Tasks

Managers can also look for ways to **enrich** an employee's role. For example, hospital cleaners who chat to patients and do tasks that help make the nurses' job easier, make a greater contribution and help create a better environment while enjoying the job more.

Carol Dweck has written extensively about the growth mindset for students and workers. You encourage a growth mindset when you:

- Set learning goals, not just performance goals
- Highlight incremental progress and
- Recognise grit (determined persistence)

Harvard Business school asked 600 managers to rank the impact on employee motivation and emotions of five workplace factors commonly thought to be effective[1]. All these factors are important, but which do you think is #1 in terms of its impact on employees?

- Recognition for good work
- Incentives
- Interpersonal support
- Support for making progress
- Clear goals

The managers ranked recognition for good work as the number one and, naturally, that is important.

However, the most impactful of these motivators, according to a multi-year study tracking the activities, motivation, and emotions of hundreds of workers, found the number one motivator for performance was the factor managers ranked last: **support for making progress.**

When people feel like they are getting somewhere and when they have support to overcome obstacles, their emotions are most positive and their drive to succeed is highest.

How you build mastery depends on your particular situation, so consider ways to set "Goldilocks tasks", enrich roles, build the growth mindset and highlight people's progress.

Purpose

Increasingly, corporates and individuals seek to "give back" by contributing to a **greater good**. Traditionally, we've had for-profit corporates and not-for-profit cooperatives or charities. A new type of organisation is emerging. One that seeks to make enough profit to be viable and sustainable, but also achieve "public good" goals.

Anita Roddick's Body Shop, gives employees paid time to volunteer—for example helping at an animal shelter or making daily phone call to elderly people living alone (the Red Cross manages the daily call program, if there is no answer they alert relatives or emergency responders).

Who Gives A Crap manufactures toilet paper, tissues, and paper towels from recycled and sustainable sources, giving half their profit to building toilets and providing access to fresh water in underdeveloped countries. Bill and Melinda Gates of Microsoft are also delivering non-water consuming toilets.

These developments are a response to the recognition that humans crave meaning and purpose in life and work.

Personality

We are all different. We have distinct personalities, tastes, and different motivations. Personality is defined as "natural patterns of thoughts, feelings and behaviours". These patterns lead us to have personal needs, wants, and values. To motivate ourselves or others, we have to find that combination of thoughts, feelings and behaviour, the needs, wants and values that provide motives that inspire the activity.

The trap we can fall into is that golden rule: "treat others as you would like to be treated yourself". The problem is, while that's good manners, it's not good motivation. That's why using instruments like the Clifton Strengths Assessment is so useful in teams. We get to learn more about our differences and how to use them in productive ways.

Old-fashioned management was based on command and control. Workers were hired hands. Wiser heads did the thinking and issued direction. Underlings merely complied and were rewarded with a pay packet. This was fine in the 19th & 20th centuries, when most work was routinely repetitious.

Today, with technology reinventing jobs, transforming workplaces and revolutionising careers. Employers exhort workers to become agile, complex problem solvers, and innovators. To achieve an excellent workforce, we have to leave traditional management practices behind and foster autonomy, mastery, and purpose.

This approach to motivation is not something you change overnight. It's going to take time to get to the point where you have confidence in them and they have confidence in you. You'll have to build trust. Train yourself and them to work with autonomy and accountability, and mentor them as we negotiate a new balance of power in the workplace.

PART IV
GUIDES

TEAM PRODUCTIVITY CHECKLIST

This checklist gives an at-a-glance guide to actions that will boost your team's productivity. How many of the ideals listed below would your people agree describe the team?

The Team Mission: We have a clear and compelling purpose. There is a reason to work together. We have a common goal, whether it is the solution to a particular problem, a challenge to be overcome or a contribution we make. Our mission inspires and appeals to our individual values.

Values: We share the ethics and ideals of the organisation. It is important to us that the place we work reflects our own character because we want to act with integrity. We want to believe that the work we do is important and makes a positive difference in the world.

Outcomes and Measures: We know what success looks like. There are specific things that are measured to show how how we are tracking. Outcomes are defined and measured and we can see the results, daily, weekly or at least monthly.

Performance Standards: We know what's expected of us. Each of us knows our role. We are clear about what to do and why it's important.

Procedures are important, but we understand it's about the outcomes rather than the process, so we can take the initiative to solve a problem or get the result. Standards of performance are clear so we can see whether we are meeting them or not.

Feedback: We get individual guidance. Praise and recognition for a job well done as well as corrective feedback and coaching are provided. We know when we're doing well and when we need to do better. We celebrate as a team when major milestones are reached. We review projects and look at what worked well, so we can repeat it; we discuss things that don't work well without blame or shame, so we can do better.

Communication and Collaboration: We have regular team meetings. We are kept well informed of what is going on in the business. We review team results, progress and problems. Our input is valued, we are encouraged to contribute ideas. We talk about the big picture as well as the day-to-day stuff. Meetings end with each of us having clear actions to implement.

Training: We are taught what we need to know. We are "onboarded" with initial training so we understand the products/services, policies and protocols of the organisation, as well as the expectations of behaviour and performance. We get regular training in knowledge and skills for our job. When things change, we are well prepared. We have formal training, on-the-job learning and sessions with internal and external specialists.

Development: Personal and Professional development is supported. We each have a personal development plan, discussed at least annually, that reflects our individual goals. Ongoing development is a priority. We can make a business case to go to conferences or relevant off-site courses. We bring such learning back to the team to share it and find ways to implement that benefit our outcomes.

Strengths: The focus is on building our strengths, not fixing weaknesses. We've learned that it's OK not to be great at everything. In the team there are some who are just naturally better in some areas and we use that to our advantage. We form partnerships that bring out our best and leverage our talents and strengths. We manage around weaknesses

Projects: We are assigned projects that develop our capabilities. When there's a challenge or an opportunity to achieve a business outcome, we discuss the goal and the reason it's important. There will be guidelines or constraints to work within. But we have freedom to develop a plan and, with approval implement it.

Belonging: We have a sense of identity, being a member of the team. We have a positive association to our group and/or our employer. People know our names, we are treated as members not numbers. We wear our badges or uniforms with pride. We talk about "we" not "they", when referring to the work-unit or organisation.

Camaraderie: There is a spirit of friendship at work. We are professional, but close relationships form. We take an interest in each other and often get to know each other well. We care about one another. We can have fun and socialise together. This helps us collaborate and cooperate in our work.

Teamwork: Everyone is important in getting the end results. Like a sports team, we have our own important role, but we need each other to get the job done. We understand how we and others fit in the team and how to work together. We are allies, we help each other out and don't let each other down.

Care: We take personal responsibility for our work. Quality matters. We have our own high standards. Excellence matters to us and we know it's not just what you do, it's the way you do it that makes the difference. Cutting corners or poor performance reflects badly on all of us and doesn't fit our self-image as a team.

Trust: We have confidence in management and they have faith in us. We are respected and treated like adults. Managers keep their promises, they don't say one thing and do another. We're all human and sometimes make mistakes but there's honest communication, they don't try to bluff. We're not overburdened with rules because it's clear what the right thing to do is.

Leadership: Leaders are our role models. They are worth following because they have a sense of direction and inspire our faith in the future. They are trustworthy and dependable, positive and strong, but compassionate. They care about us as people. They share important information with us so we know where the organisation is headed and how it's doing. Because of this transparency we feel secure—if there are problems they'll give us the heads up in time to do something about it.

This is an extract from my ebook: *How to Lift Team Productivity* .You can **download a free copy** here: https://dl.bookfunnel.com/ji85sra3yc

BRAINSTORMING

Brainstorming is a technique that can be used by yourself or with others to harness creativity to generate alternatives or solutions.

The process involves listing as many ideas as possible, without judging their viability or worth, then choosing those most likely to produce the result you want.

Keys to brainstorming success:

1. Clearly define the purpose, issue, or problem you want to solve
2. List some criteria for a successful solution, for example: a plan that could be implemented with the resources available and in a specified timeframe.
3. Have individuals brainstorm alone first, then as a group
4. Aim for quantity of ideas not quality—no idea is too silly, unusual, and novel ideas are welcome
5. Collect the ideas and display them so they are visible to the group
6. Nobody should comment or critique any ideas until all that can be thought of by the group are listed

7. Review the ideas, see if you can build on them, combine them or improve them
8. Now you can evaluate ideas against the criteria for a successful solution listed at the beginning
9. Choose the best result or combination of ideas and plan how to implement it.

FORCE FIELD ANALYSIS

Here is a team process that can be very illuminating. Developed by Kurt Lewin, force-field analysis will engage your team in identifying driving forces—factors that support, encourage or propel people toward the desired situation and restraining forces — all the factors, pressures and issues that restrict progress or prevent the desired situation. Once identified, you can work to reduce restraining forces and boost driving forces.

To do a force-field analysis, you will need a space for the team to get together, flip chart paper on the wall and marker pens. Then:

1. Discuss and succinctly define the team outcome you want to improve. Write this on a flip chart as the desired situation—where we want to be.
2. Discuss and briefly describe the current situation—where we are now. List this on another sheet, place to the left of the first.
3. Brainstorm a list of restraining forces - factors that hinder or work against people achieving the desired outcome.

4. Brainstorm a list of driving forces—things that help or would increase their ability to accomplish the desired outcome.
5. Illustrate the strength of each of the forces working for and against you by agreeing an impact rating of 1-5 (5 is strongest) and drawing an arrow toward or away from the outcome of a corresponding length.
6. Then have the team suggest actions that could increase each driving force and decrease the impact of each restraining force.
7. Sort out the most practical ideas and what's easy to implement, decide priorities and create a team action plan.

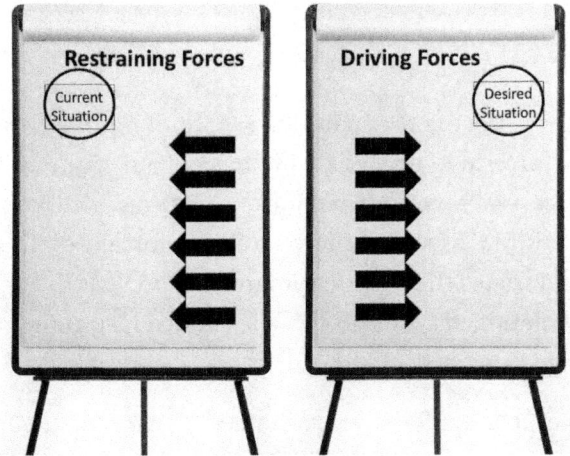

Figure 39: Force-field Analysis

You can use force-field analysis in any group (or by yourself) for any goal.

Try force-field analysis on one of your own goals. Then use it on a performance goal specific to your team.

MINDMAPPING

A mindmap is related to spidergrams and mud maps—it is a visual representation of connected ideas. Often, it's done on large sheets of paper, a whiteboard or with computer software. Frequently, it is colourful and consists of words in circles and connected with arrows and sometimes pictures and diagrams.

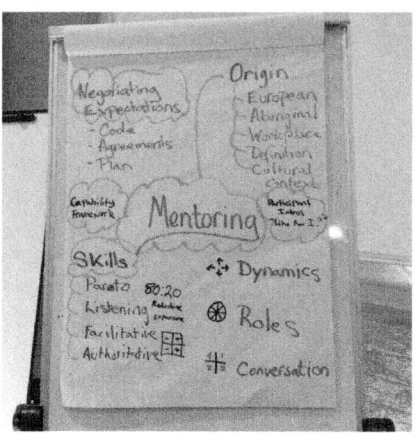

Mindmap Outline of a Mentoring Workshop

Mind maps are used for planning, as an aid to summarising and retaining learning, and as a brainstorming technique. I use a mindmap as the starting point for writing presentations, workshops, articles and books.

Steps

1. Write the topic, keyword, or phrase in the centre of a large sheet of paper
2. Generate 4 or 5 main ideas and list them evenly spaced around the central idea. Draw lines or arrows from the central keyword to connect these main ideas (like spider's legs)
3. List supporting details, ideas, topics, questions or tasks for each of the main ideas
4. Connect each main idea to its supporting details with lines or arrows
5. Add pictures and diagrams to assist recall and summarise details

MENTOR MASTER CLASSES

Your purchase of this book includes access to Mentor Master Class videos and worksheets.

1. Why Master Mentoring?
2. Build Trust
3. A Structure for Mentoring Conversations
4. How do you Find the Time to Mentor?
5. How Mentors Leverage Mentoring
6. Critical, Creative and Reflective Listening
7. Listen Well
8. Good Question
9. Goal Getting
10. Hidden Talent
11. Mastering Motivation

12. Strengths-based Development

Access them here: http://mentoring-works.com/mentor-master-classes/

Use the password:

MMCAR2021

NOTES

10. Feedback

1. Kluger, Avraham & DeNisi, Angelo. (1996). *The Effects of Feedback Interventions on Performance: A Historical Review, a Meta-Analysis, and a Preliminary Feedback Intervention Theory.* Psychological Bulletin. 119. 254-284. 10.1037/0033-2909.119.2.254.
2. *The Most Expensive Mistake Leaders Can Make.* Gallup Business Journal
3. David Rock *Give Your Performance Management System a Review.* Harvard Business Rev
4. Bryant Ott (2018) 3 reasons Why Performance Development Wins in the Workplace. Gallup Business Journal
5. Shawn Achor (2012) Positive Intelligence. Harvard Business Review
6. https://www.youtube.com/watch?v=azbRhVCt8Rw

11. Motivation

1. https://hbr.org/2010/01/the-hbr-list-breakthrough-ideas-for-2010

ABOUT THE AUTHOR

Ann Rolfe has over 30 years' experience in adult learning, career coaching and mentoring. She is a trained career counsellor, certified Gallup Strengths Coach and Australia's most published author on mentoring.

Ann Rolfe has spoken international conferences in Australia, Canada, China, The Philippines, Singapore, and USA. She has run workshops for people in fields as diverse as health, construction, energy, communications, education, law, and government. She runs regular webinars that are attended by participants all over the world

She has developed award-winning mentoring programs for Aboriginal people and facilitated programs for women, graduates and injured people mentored by Paralympians.

Contact ann@mentoring-works.com

Join the Mentoring Works Facebook group here:

https://www.facebook.com/groups/2106516549583612/

Sign up for invitations to our free webinars here:

https://mentoring-works.us2.list-manage.com/subscribe?u=1a30d07bcf6f8ec3bc5a9da15&id=19b3cbec71

ALSO BY ANN ROLFE

Thousands of people have become better mentors using these books. The mentoring process described is not complicated, it's completely flexible and versatile in any type of mentoring situation. The proven techniques have been used in mentoring for professionals, graduates and students in health, construction, energy, communications, education, law and government.

Mentor and Mentoring Mindset, Skills and Tools 4th edition

Written for both for mentors and mentees, so you can literally be on the same page. It is based on decades of experience and explains the essential ingredients of mentoring conversations and relationships that work. See content and details here: http://mentoring-works.com/mentoring-mindset-skills-and-tools/

The Mentor's Toolkit for Career Conversations

An in-depth description of a four-step method for leading a mentoring conversation focussed on career, with examples of questions, thought-starters, and discussion topics. Purchase includes access to online video career planning course and 45 reproducible activities. Find out more here: http://mentoring-works.com/the-mentors-toolkit-for-career-conversations/

Not a Random Chat - Life Skills to Learn with a Mentor

Coming soon

Printed in Great Britain
by Amazon